SUCCESSONALITY

The ten secrets to building a success-focused personality

ANDREEA VANACKER

Copyright © 2010 by 9101-3698 Quebec Inc.

All rights reserved. No part of this book may be reproduced, copied, stored, or transmitted in any form or by any means (graphic, electronic, or mechanical, including photocopying, recording, or information storage and retrieval systems) without the prior written permission from the publisher.

Published by 9101-3698 Quebec Inc.

ISBN: 978-0-9813631-0-3

Printed in United States of America

Cover Design by Catherine Savard

Second Edition

To my daughter, since you are my source of inspiration for this book.

To life!
To creation!
To celebrations!

Success [*suh*-k-ses]: The favorable or prosperous termination of anything attempted (Webster's Revised Unabridged Dictionary). Attainment of wealth, favor or eminence (Merriam-Webster Dictionary).

•

Personality [pur-*suh*-nal-i-tee]: The totality of an individual's behavioral and emotional tendencies. The organization of the individual's distinguishing character traits, attitudes, or habits (Merriam-Webster's Medical Dictionary).

•

Successonality [*suh*-k-ses-o-nal-i-tee]: The behaviors and habits of individuals that are focused on achieving extraordinary outcomes in every undertaking, and in leading a fulfilling and successful life (Andreea Vanacker).

If you are on a quest to a higher level of achievement and extraordinary results; if you are searching for solutions on how to change your habits in order to turn your dreams into reality and become successful, then this book is for you.

Build your Successonality today!

TABLE OF CONTENTS

	Page
Inspiration for this book	3
Chapter 1. Chief Life Officer	10
Chapter 2. Discipline of Action	22
Chapter 3. Power of Persistence	30
Chapter 4. Self-Confidence	40
Chapter 5. Excellence	50
Chapter 6. Dare	58
Chapter 7. Seize the Moment	66
Chapter 8. Creativity & Passion	76
Chapter 9. Self Development	84
Chapter 10. Positive Attitude	96
Final reflections	106
Begin your journey & share your story	108
About the Author	113

INSPIRATION FOR THIS BOOK

Since our daughter has blossomed into our lives, I began searching for ways to instill in her love, true virtue, moral goodness, generosity, creativity and joy. To the best of my ability, I share with her everyday examples of my experiences and teach her to turn her own experience to a joyful one. Reflecting on this topic, I decided to write this book for her, and along the way, the idea of sharing it with others dawned on me. *"The great use of life is to spend it for something that will outlast it,"* said the great psychologist and philosopher William James. Sharing our knowledge is the best gift we can give the generations to come.

As I was contemplating about what insights I could share with my daughter, I never imagined how much I could learn from a three-year-old about life. Her essence is so pure and innocent that she embodies the elements of a happy and successful life, elements that we often overlook as we get older. Observing her behavior, I became aware of the traits which formed the foundation and inspiration for this book, and which I would like to share with you.

- **Mission & persistence**: It never seizes to amaze me how persevering a child can be when on a mission to achieve a goal. When our daughter was learning to walk, she proudly pushed the walker forward step by step, and if I tried to help her, she would push me away. Even when she was already walking and would occasionally fall, it was not an impediment, as she was adamant to succeed on her own. She would stand up and continue to walk without our help. This was *her* mission, and she was determined to find her way. The pleasure of being independent and free, of no longer having to rely on anyone, fueled her determination. She applied the same determination to every new activity, whether it was riding a tricycle, learning to swim, or riding a small white pony. When she started using her tricycle, she was open to advice on improving her skill, but if we helped too much, she would get upset and say she wanted to do it on her own. To her, falling down once in a while was part of the learning process. She demonstrated the same tenacity with any new experience. If she was on a mission, nothing could stop her from succeeding! Imagine that every move you make leads you to achieve a set goal and that nothing can stop you from succeeding. Imagine a world of endless possibilities that can be realized through persistence.

- **Enjoying the moment**: Everything our daughter does each day is about full enjoyment and pleasure. Scientists have found that children spend almost half their day laughing, while adults spend only a tiny fraction of their day doing the same. Young children do not reflect on the past or worry about the future; they live fully in the present moment. Diversity and intense curiosity are the key to a child's enjoyment. Because children get bored quickly, they will rarely spend hours on one specific activity. Their true pleasure comes from a balance of diverse activities that allow them to develop their intellectual, creative and physical capabilities. The lesson for all of us is to indulge in activities that bring pleasure, to laugh more, play more and to have a positive outlook on life.

- **The pleasure of discovery**: Spending a few hours with a child can sharpen one's awareness of the surroundings. A walk in the park becomes a re-discovery of nature's beauty. Your attention focuses on every flower and every tree, every birdcall, every animal and even the tiniest insect. The pleasure children get from looking at everything around them with joy and amazement is astonishing. Examining a flower will provide more than pleasure for the eyes. All senses are engaged as a child's natural curiosity is aroused by the smell, touch and sometimes even the urge to taste. There is enormous satisfaction and excitement to a child when learning a new word, a musical instrument, the alphabet or a new game. A child at the age of one-and-a-half learns approximately six new words per day. Imagine how we can grow and develop if we expanded our skills by a small fraction each day. Imagine how your life would improve if you look beyond all ordinary things to find beauty, experience new sensations and discover new opportunities. Imagine the endless possibilities if not a moment is wasted but rather each opportunity for growth is savored as we strive towards our goals.

- **Fearlessness**: In a young child's quest for discovery and growth, taking risks becomes part of the game. When it comes to new and creative activities, imagination rules. Sometimes our daughter would engage in dangerous undertakings, all with a smile on her face. If I showed concern or fear that she might get hurt, she started laughing. She was proud of herself for tackling a new challenge. When she began mastering a new skill, she introduced minor variations; doing the same thing but in a more difficult position, like standing on one foot while throwing something; or riding her tricycle with one hand. She simply loves challenges. Children do not foresee danger in their activities, they focus on the positive outcome and the pure pleasure they experience in the process. They enjoy risky pursuits because they know they will have more fun along the way and greater satisfaction in the end.

Try to start looking at new challenges in your life in the same way. Fear will prevent you from moving forward if too much concentration on what one has to lose from the process prevails. Imagine the endless opportunities you might discover if you focus on the best-case scenario rather than on your fear.

- **The "No!" factor**: Everybody warns parents about the "terrible two" — the stage around the age of two, when children develop their independence and opinions, and "No!" becomes their favorite word. Although this stage can be exhausting, parents should appreciate that toddlers are simply developing their personality and they are determined to get what they want because it feels right to them. A two-year-old will not say "Yes!" to please others. Their world is about *them* and their pleasure. As our daughter was going through this period, I asked myself whether I could learn from her how to stand up for myself. How many times have we all made decisions that made others happy rather than asked ourselves if it would make sense to us. We can also look at the "No!" stage as a challenge. I for one believe in never taking "No!" for an answer if one really wants to achieve a goal. On many occasions my belief and persistence paid off.

  Finally, as parents, we learned how to use our creativity in addressing and turning our daughter's "No!" to a "Yes!" We did this by explaining to her other options, helping her see new perspectives that she may have overlooked, and by giving her the freedom to make her own choices.

- **The "Why?" period**: After the "No!" period, comes the "Why?" At this phase, which happens around the age of three, the child is able to verbally communicate and can begin a dialogue with others. Our daughter frequently asked questions like: "Why is the sky blue and the sun yellow?"; "How do plants grow?" or "Where is the moon tonight?" Each of our responses led to a more in-depth questioning which shed a new light on my own life. It gave me an incentive to ask myself a series of similar questions about myself, the importance of people in my life, about what I was doing and why.

Imagine taking time each day to reflect on your life, and the actions to take towards your goals by asking yourself similar questions: "Why am I doing this?" and "Why is this important for me?" Every moment is valuable. Don't let your life pass you by. Ask yourself regularly what your intentions are and if you are heading in the right direction. There is no limit to how many "Whys" you can ask yourself.

- **No limits**: When I look at our daughter, I think not of limitations but rather of endless possibilities. I am amazed by the limitless potential children have. They are like sponges, they learn quickly. My husband and I debated whether to expose our daughter to different languages or to master one before introducing others later. After researching on the subject and consulting with psychologists, we decided to expose her to three languages simultaneously. By the age of three, she could converse in all three effortlessly. If you were to imagine a life without limits, what actions and decisions would you make today?

Picasso used to say *"Every child is an artist. The problem is how to remain an artist once he grows up."* For me, the word *artist* evokes creativity, imagination and persistence in making real what one imagines. This book is about sharing key insights to live an extraordinary life and to encourage you to create the canvas of your life. Individuals with enormous success share similar traits in terms of personality and attitude. I truly believe that any individual can build the habits required to succeed personally and professionally. I call this "Successonality" and there are ten key elements that make up a personality focused on success and achievement. We are creators of our own destiny, and everyone is capable of achieving a great and successful life. To reach your highest potential in everything you pursue, follow the guidelines described in the following chapters and let your brilliance shine.

Your extraordinary life begins now!

CHIEF LIFE OFFICER

Think Big. Pursue your dreams.

"Great minds have purposes, others have wishes." – WASHINGTON IRVING (1783-1859)

"The secret of success is constancy of purpose." – BENJAMIN DISRAELI (1804-1881)

"Go confidently in the direction of your dreams. Live the life you have imagined." – HENRY DAVID THOREAU (1817-1876)

Before you begin any journey, you need to decide where you would like to go. You cannot take action to execute your plans unless you have a vision and clear goals. Whether your goal is to become a millionaire, or to reach an ideal weight, you need to have clarity about when, where, and how you want to achieve that goal.

Setting a vision for where you would like to take your life, professionally or personally, begins with a dream. Victor Hugo said that *"there is nothing like a dream to create the future."* You have the power to change your life as much or as little as you decide. You have the power to decide how successful you can be. You can achieve what seems unachievable, but you must first believe that this is possible, and be ready to put all your energy in turning any dream into reality. Madonna, Bill Clinton and Oprah Winfrey are good examples of role models. They started their careers from difficult circumstances to achieving greatness. Do not let your current status dictate where you will be in the future. If you believe you can achieve greatness, you will find the way. **Think big! Act!**

Remember the following wise advice by Mark Twain (1835-1910):

> *"Twenty years from now, you will be more disappointed by the things you didn't do than by the ones you did. So throw off the bowlines. Sail away from the safe harbor. Catch the trade winds in your sails. Explore. Dream. Discover."*

The person who is forever looking everywhere to see what may turn up never finds anything. If one looks for nothing in particular, one finds just that and nothing more. We find what we wholeheartedly seek. To generate happy circumstances with magnificent proportions, your life purpose must be well-defined.

In the corporate milieu, we often speak about **leaders** and **followers**. Leaders are the individuals who have a vision for their business. They tend to excite and engage others to pursue, as a team, specific goals towards full execution and success. **Leadership on the personal level is about taking control of your life.** It is about deciding where you want to go, when, how, and why, rather than letting others decide for you. If you want to succeed and to have a happy and fulfilling life, you need to be the architect and to lay out your life's plans and foundations that will lead you to materialize your ultimate goal.

It has often been debated whether leaders are born or made. Having spent over fifteen years in the corporate world, I assure you that **leaders can be made. It all starts with initiative and desire.** As you can learn a new language, or become proficient in a specific discipline, you can acquire leadership skills through seminars, courses, coaching and hands-on experience. Great leaders can work effectively with people with different personalities, cultures and motivational levels. An excellent leader will realize that applying the same management principles to all employees and hoping to achieve the same results will not work. In order to achieve desired results, leaders find the key to what makes an individual employee tick, what makes him or her motivated and happy. They then adapt their communication and management style to different personalities. From my own professional experience, I consider this absolutely essential when managing international teams of different backgrounds and cultures. Through experience, and making mistakes, new insights will emerge and will enable you to become a stronger leader. As Confucius (551 BC – 479 BC) said *"I hear and I forget. I see and I remember. I do and I understand."* Practice will bring new insights and sharpness to your skills. You cannot master them by simply reading a book or learning theories.

As Chief Executive Officers lead companies, you need to lead your life, and become your own Chief Life Officer. **Personal leadership is about having clear goals, choosing your life's mission, and working with others to help you with your journey.** To achieve this, networking is essential. In order to receive true assistance from others, you must first provide assistance and help these individuals become successful. *"Give and you shall receive"* - this rule from the Gospel is never to be forgotten. When you contact someone you know, do not ask what *they* can do for you, but rather what *you* can do for them. Be proactive, introduce someone you have met to someone you think may be resourceful and interesting to meet. Networking is about generosity. Everything that goes around, comes around.

To take your life to new heights and to be a great Chief Life Officer, you have to **think big** and pursue challenging targets. Thinking big implies looking beyond the position you are in today, and imagining phenomenal results you can achieve in order to become the best among the best. **Your future successes will not only depend on the clarity of your goals, but also on your belief that you can achieve greatness**. If you are truly committed to taking your life to the next level, then engage in impressive projects. Why aim for the national championships when you can aim for gold at the Olympics? While you are training to compete for a gold medal, focus on perfecting your skills not in multiple disciplines, but rather in one only. If you split your effort into many disciplines, you will not succeed. Focus is the key to reaching your goal. In spite of adversity, focus will give you strength to move forward. For inspiration, let us examine young children once again. When babies are learning to walk, their focus is so strong on walking that they may not progress in other areas, such as speech development. Once they master a skill, they move on to the next challenge. This learning process can be applied to every challenge you decide to undertake.

The great difference between those who succeed and those who fail as Chief Life Officers consists not in the amount of work done, but in the amount of **work done intelligently**. Many of those who fail in one area may be building things with one hand only to tear them down with the other. They do not grasp circumstances and change them into opportunities. They have no faculty of turning defeats into victories. A one-talent person who decides upon a definite project accomplishes more than a five-talent person who scatters his or her energies, and never knows exactly what to do. The weakest living creature, by concentrating its powers upon one thing, can accomplish something; the strongest, by dispersing its strengths over many, may fail to accomplish anything.

A few years ago, I decided to pursue a Ph.D. because I was aiming to work for the IMF or World Bank, and the requirement for the position was a doctorate. At the time, it seemed to me like an impossible dream, filled with many unknowns because I chose to do my studies in Europe. The journey was filled with many challenges and I often contemplated pulling out. The difficulty laid not only in the rigor and discipline that was required to write the dissertation, but in the realization I came to in the middle of my studies that I no longer wanted to work with development issues for either of those organizations, but rather to run businesses, which is my true passion. My original dream evolved into a personal challenge that led to a greater significance for me. Getting my Ph.D. in Economics was no longer about pursuing the career path I was originally interested in, but rather a personal challenge. I was determined to prove to myself that I could succeed in getting the degree. I felt that if I completed my Ph.D., it would help my career and become a passport for future endeavors. Once I had established this belief, my focus and energy was to get to the finish line. I also dramatically changed the rules for the dissertation in terms of content - I expanded the thesis beyond theoretical economic models to integrate specific examples of success stories taken from the business world. In addition, I persuaded a French University to accept my dissertation in English. In the University's history, this had never been done.

Your body and soul need to be committed to achieving extraordinary results. Take control of your life, embrace your role as Chief Life Officer, and decide what your next big accomplishment should be. Set short-term targets that you can track, measure and celebrate. No matter how difficult the journey, never lose focus or hope.

Begin this process by setting **SMART-P²** goals:

- **Specific**: in order to achieve a goal, you need to be very specific about what you are trying to achieve. Do not say, "I want to lose weight," but rather "I want to lose five pounds by the end of the month." Instead of saying, "I would like to earn more money," be more specific by stating "I would like to earn one million dollars by the end of this year." Start by setting realistic goals to begin the process. When you reach your first goals, set higher and more aggressive objectives. Set one goal at a time, and focus on achieving it. Split your goals into professional and personal categories, and you can even sub-segment these further for greater clarity. As for personal goals, you can focus on your health, your relationships/marriage, your children, your social network or personal development. Your professional goals may be financial or career achievements. Divide each section of these goals into subsections, and ask yourself the following questions:
    - What do I want to achieve in the long term?
    - What would I consider success?
    - What would I consider achieving vs. exceeding my objectives?
    - What is my ideal wish list for this sub-goal in the short term and long term?
- **Measurable**: If you cannot effectively track and measure your progress from start to finish, your goal needs to be revisited. When doing this, you need to set short-term targets that will help you achieve your ultimate goal. Achieving these interim goals will give you the confidence to continue until the finish line. This strategy will also allow you to realign your execution strategy at the end of each

one of your mini-milestones in order to increase your probability of success.
- **Actionable**: Set goals that you can take action on right away; otherwise, your goal will become an unfulfilled dream before you even start. Do not wait for tomorrow or next week. Execution is key to your success.
- **Relevant**: Set goals that are important to you, and that are aligned with who you would ultimately like to become in the future. This is not about what your parents, partner or husband/wife expects you to do, but rather what feels right for you now. If you have always dreamed of winning a marathon, start by building your plan today.
- **Time bound**: All goals need to be time bound in order to be truly achievable. If you simply say "I would love one day to have a house on the beach," you will end up at retirement saying "I would have loved to have a house on the beach." Instead, say, "I will start saving 10% of my salary over the next two years in order to buy my beach house by the time I am 45."
- **Prioritize**: If you split your goals into personal and professional goals, which I highly recommend, you must establish a priority list in terms of what is the most important goal for you to achieve in the immediate term. This does not mean that you will aim to achieve one goal to the detriment of another, such as focusing on your professional goals to the detriment of your personal ones. Prioritization allows you to focus your energy in the areas that are most important for you now, in order to avoid scattering your efforts.
- **Plan**: For every goal you have set, you must develop a written action plan to achieve intermediate steps that will ultimately lead you to achieve your goal.

This will become your recipe for success. Build your action plan over a set period of time, with interim tasks and targets. If this requires that you build specific skills, or seek advice from a specialist, include this as part of your action plan. Take clear actions each day without any excuses if you truly want to move forward. To help you in this process, write down your Chief Life Officer vision and action plan. This will force you to have clarity on your goal. The following chapter will provide additional insights on prioritization and the importance of continued and constructive action, which I call "discipline of action."

By combining all the above guidelines you can go from dream to reality. As the Chinese proverbs states, *"a journey of a thousand miles begins with one step."* Take this step forward today, and do not look back.

> *"The important thing in life is to have a great aim, and to possess the aptitude and perseverance to attain it."* —JOHANN WOLFGANG VON GOETHE (1749-1832)

Many historical figures changed the face of the world by having one purpose, one objective, one aim. Napoleon is a great example. He did not waste time balancing the probabilities of failure or success, or delayed his purpose. There was no veering off his course and no dreaming away time. He maintained one vision and purpose straight to his goal.

To succeed, you must concentrate all the faculties of your mind upon one aim, and have tenacity until victory.

Every other inclination, which tempts you from your aim, must be suppressed. Countless great men and women have been noted for their powers of concentration, which make them oblivious of everything outside their aim. One great example is Victor Hugo, who wrote his "Notre Dame" during the revolution of 1830, while the noise of bombs and bullets were nearby.

Those who dissipate their efforts may compromise their progress and ultimate success. Those who focus on one thing often succeed. Some great examples in this area are Edison, Columbus, Morse, Bell, and Watt. Edward Gibbon dedicated twenty years to *"The History of the Decline and Fall of the Roman Empire"*. Cyrus West Field crossed the ocean fifty times to lay a cable, while everyone challenged him. Newton wrote his "*Chronology of Ancient Nations*" sixteen times. A more recent example is Jeff Bezos, CEO of Amazon.com. Although the company struggled in achieving profitability in the early years, Jeff Bezos stayed focused on popularizing online shopping, and achieved his goal brilliantly. Lance Armstrong also marveled the world by winning the Tour de France seven consecutive times, after having survived cancer.

A great purpose is cumulative, and, like a great magnet, it attracts favorable circumstances. If you have one idea, a single and intense purpose, you will cut your way through obstacles and forge to the front. **Concentration is the keynote of success**. If you often have intermittent attacks of enthusiasm for doing many great things at the same time, but your zeal evaporates before you decide what to do, start focusing on one thing at a time. You must conquer your conflicting motives, and have the power to choose one goal and persevere with a single aim, sacrificing every interfering inclination. One talent focused in a single direction will accomplish infinitely more than many talents scattered. This is the secret of a great Chief Life Officer.

The men and women who have changed the world have focused on a single aim that they pursued passionately. This allowed them to be recognized as discoverers of new lands, scientific breakthroughs and new inventions that have changed our lives. A wavering aim, a faltering purpose, has led many to regret not having achieved much. There is an old Oriental saying that states – *"he who runs after two rabbits at the same time will catch neither."* It is the single aim that wins. If you want to succeed, you need an action plan and focus. You must set your course and adhere to it. Focus on the goal, and do not divert course every time a difficulty is thrown in your path. Be creative in finding solutions to overcome challenges and never lose hope.

As Chief Executive Officers of companies focus on building a core expertise in a specific area, as a Chief Life Officer you need to train yourself to do one thing as well as it can be done. Only then can you stand out in terms of achievement, irrespective of your education level. You can identify your greatest strengths by reflecting on the things that you are best at, and that also provide you the most joy. As you think about your interests and past experiences, think about what energizes you and what demoralizes you. The activities that give you the most energy are in general the ones that best leverage your key strengths and natural talents. Never aim to be a jack-of-all-trades, since the constant changing of occupation is fatal to all success. Half-learned trades, even if you have twenty, will never give you a good living, much less a competency. However, if you have been in a line of business that you do not enjoy or are not good at, and you feel you have a calling in a different domain, pursue it with all your strength and dedication. But make sure that deep down you know this is the path you want to engage in for many years to come. Explore it, test it out, and learn everything imaginable before moving forward. Look into www.vocationvacations.com, a site that allows you to test out a possible new career before making a career switch. Alternatively, volunteer your time to companies in the line of work you want to pursue to really determine if you are heading in the right direction. I can tell you from my own experience that this is extremely useful. When I was in college, my parents wanted one of their three children to become a doctor. Given that my two older brothers had pursued different paths, their hope was fully focused on me to become one. After signing up for a Health Science degree, in which my days were filled with biology, chemistry and physics courses, I realized I did not really enjoy this field. Before completely closing the door on the medical field, I decided to experience the work hands on in a hospital environment. After exploring various areas, I closed the door forever on medicine. My gut feeling was that this field was not for me, and decided to invest in my entrepreneurial spirit and language skills, and to pursue a path in international business. This is where my heart was then and still is today.

Ensure your purposes are clear and your aims are constant, and no matter what difficulties you may encounter, have faith that you will succeed. As great Chief Executive Officers lead companies to success with clarity and tenacity, you must aim to become a fantastic Chief Life Officer who takes your life to new heights. Determine your purpose in life, pursue it with courage and never lose sight of your goal until it is achieved. Take control of your destiny today, and make your life a truly rewarding and fulfilling adventure. You are more powerful than you think!

DISCIPLINE OF ACTION

Actions speak louder than words.

"You can't cross a sea by merely staring into the water" – RABINDRANATH TAGORE (1841-1944)

"An ounce of action is worth a ton of theory" – FRIEDRICH ENGELS (1820-1895)

"However brilliant an action, it should not be esteemed great unless the result of a great motive" – FRANCOIS DE LA ROCHEFOUCAULD (1613-1680)

Global leaders in all industries are not only recognized for the vision and clarity of their main goals, but for their prompt and firm decision making, and for taking action. When you decide to become a great Chief Life Officer and establish your goals, the discipline of continuous and focused action will be the key to your success. **Actions speak louder than words.** Without action, words and plans will evaporate. Men and women who have left their mark have made the habit of prompt decisions and actions. An undecided person who is forever balancing between two opinions, or debating which of two courses to take, predicates no control over themselves, and allows others to make decisions for them. The person who makes decisions promptly, does not wait for favorable circumstances, and does not submit to external events.

When you set up your action plan to achieve your personal or professional dreams, unforeseen and unplanned circumstances which seem out of your control can emerge at any time. The power to decide instantly on the best course of action in these situations, and to sacrifice every opposing motive, is the most potent force in being successful. To hesitate is to lose. The person who procrastinates, weighing and balancing all options, will not accomplish much. This attitude does not build confidence, it invites mistrust. The individual, who makes clear decisions and has direction, has power. When asked the secret to his success, Alexander the Great proclaimed that he conquered the world "*by not wavering.*"

If you want to acquire the action habit, you must **take action even at times of unfavorable circumstances**. Conditions will rarely be perfect at the starting point or during the process. Be recognized as a doer, rather than someone who says you will do something and never does. Action will bring you greater strength and confidence, while lack of action will fuel your fears. Through concrete action, inspiration will rise, and progress will be easier. Think of it like getting on a bicycle. The first push may seem hard, but once you are on a roll, the action seems effortless.

As you pursue your goals, various opportunities may come your way. However, great opportunities not only come seldom into the most fortunate life, but also are often quickly gone. Without promptness, no success is possible. The decided person not only has the advantage of the time saved from procrastination, but also saves energy and vital force.

Every person may at some time or another come across tremendous life difficulties, at times almost overwhelming. Do not doubt yourself every time you come to a hard place in life, since this will not lead to success. Without decision and action, there can be no concentration. To succeed, you must concentrate. **If you dissipate your energy and scatter your forces, you will execute nothing.** You will not be able to hold on to one thing long enough to bring success out of it. If one day you pursue a project, or a specific vocation, because you feel it is the right thing you want to do, and the next day your enthusiasm evaporates, and you drop it to pursue another, you run the risk of continuously vacillating through life. By pursuing any new project that happens to appeal to you as the most desirable at the time, without using your judgment or common sense, you will be unable to drive forward a project to completion. Do not throw away all the skill and experience you have acquired in mastering your profession, since you will never reach the stage of competency, comfort, and contentment required to achieve your goal.

Do not be bewildered and dazed whenever a responsibility is thrust upon you to make an important decision. The very effort to come to an immediate decision brings on all sorts of doubts, difficulties and fears, obliterating the courage required to attempt to remove the obstacles. **Lack of action, and hesitation, are fatal to progress, fatal to success**. Do not fall into the analysis paralysis mode, where you are continuously deliberating, weighing, considering, pondering, but never acting. *Putting off* usually means leaving off, and *going to do* becomes did not do. Opportunities may slip through your fingers and may not emerge again in the future. A few minutes often makes all the difference between victory and defeat, success and failure. Discipline of action is crucial to your success. Commit yourself, in spite of unforeseen challenges and priorities that may come into your life, to **have the discipline to not let your long-term goals and dreams be compromised by short-term life realities.** If you set yourself a deadline to achieve a specific goal, do everything to achieve it. Remember that you are your Chief Life Officer, and that if you do not instill discipline in your daily life, you will struggle to pursue your dreams. Discipline is about keeping the commitment you made to yourself. Find ways that work for you. Make your commitments public on sites such as www.pledgehammer.com if you think that would help you keep them.

There are critical moments in achieving success. If you hesitate, or become lazy, all could be lost. When you are faced with this situation, apply the following guidelines:

- **The Regret Question**: When you are having a difficult time deciding what action to take, ask yourself the following question: "Will I regret this decision if I took this action now or in the future?", and only you can define the timeframe for the future and whether it is measured in days, weeks, months or years. All you have to do is answer "yes" or "no" each time. By doing this, you begin focusing on the implications of your actions, and begin determining whether your decision makes sense or not, and whether or not you can live with it now and in the future. In certain circumstances, you may only have a few seconds to answer this question, and it may take longer in other cases.
- **Reality of time**: Ask yourself the following questions every time you start getting lazy or feel that your discipline for action is being compromised:
  - By what age do I wish to reach my dreams?
  - How much time do I really think I have left to reach my objectives?
  - Am I truly living my life, and making the most of it, or is life just passing me by?

  Many people live their lives as if they will live forever, and often feel that they have plenty of time in the future to allow them the luxury of pushing their projects or dreams to tomorrow. They believe that death is a distant reality, and there is no rush for

great accomplishments. Imagine you are one of these people. What if you looked backwards at your life, and began thinking about your true life expectancy based on your life style, and then asked yourself how much time you truly have left to achieve specific goals. How many years do you want to live without a true-life purpose and without a true sense of accomplishment? Do not waste a single moment in getting closer to your dreams, and do not take time for granted. Time is a precious gift for those who know how to make the most of it. Use your time wisely before it is too late.

- **Prioritization:** Start each day by defining what your "3 Most Important Priorities" are to get closer to your goal. No matter what comes your way during the day, you have to achieve your "3 Most Important Priorities." Managing your time right is the key to progress and ultimate success. This requires continuous discipline.
- **Expand your comfort zone**: Remaining within your comfort zone can appear to be a secure way to protect yourself in the future, but in reality you are creating boundaries that stop you from opening yourself to new opportunities and new challenges. Evolution and change are key to future survival, and if you create your vision but lack action and an openness to change, the future will be less promising.
- **Action plan**: Once a decision is made to pursue a certain track, you must build an action plan to push things forward to full completion, and true success. Segment your actions in small achievable targets that are time bound and measurable. Celebrate the achievement of key milestones and keep pressing forward irrespective of obstacles or crises that emerge. In challenging times, you must look at

managing your risks while not overlooking opportunities. By finding this balance, you will find success.

- **Smart work vs. hard work**: The discipline of action requires that you think intelligently before you act. Working *hard* to pursue a dream without working *smart* will not lead you closer to realizing it. You must be effective and efficient at the same time. "Effective" means producing an intended result or reaching a specific goal, while "efficient" signifies acting in the best possible manner and leveraging your knowledge to pursue a specific purpose with the least waste of time, effort and expense. If you are struggling to find ways to work smart, seek advice from a good mentor or an expert *before* you begin engaging on the path to your dream.
- **Act NOW:** Waiting for the best circumstances before taking action will always prevent you from moving forward. By acting now, you will relieve your fears and gain confidence. The words "act NOW" should replace words such as "tomorrow," "next week" or "next month." Put yourself in the place that allows you to take the first step now. If you need to start a specific activity, such as writing a report, then get in front of the computer or take a pen and paper out; or if you must call a key client, then pick up the phone and start dialing the number. Life is too short to leave to tomorrow what you can take action on NOW.

> *"Whatever you can do or dream you can, begin it. Boldness has genius, power and magic in it. Begin it now."*- JOHANN WOLFGANG VON GOETHE (1740-1832)

POWER OF PERSISTENCE

Failure is not an option.

> *"Our greatest glory is not in never falling, but in getting up every time we do"* – CONFUCIUS (551 – 479 BC)

> *"You gain strength, courage and confidence by every experience if you really stop to look fear in the face. You are able to say to yourself, 'I have lived through this…I can take the next thing that comes along.' You must do the thing you think you cannot do."* –ELEANOR ROOSEVELT (1884-1962)

> *"Victory belongs to the most persevering"* – NAPOLEON BONAPARTE (1769-1821)

I was exposed to the importance of persistence when I was very young. During the communist regime in Eastern Europe, my parents wanted to leave for a better life in Canada. My parents insisted that the entire family leave the country together and within the rule of law. However, expressing a desire to leave a communist country is an explicit demonstration that one is against the regime, a viewpoint which was considered unacceptable. Over a period of more than a year, while my parents went to the government office every single day to ensure that our request was being processed, attempts were made to harm both my parents without success. My parents were eventually demoted professionally and they were assigned to a remote location, in order to create a huge distance between the government offices and their new location. My brothers and I were denied access to schooling, and we knew that we were constantly being monitored. In spite of all the hardships we experienced in this process, my parents knew and many times said that "the children will have a brighter future abroad." They never gave up, despite the many creative measures the authorities deployed in an attempt to change our minds. When we were finally granted our passports, we had the liberty to leave legally. This was for us the true victory we always hoped for. But this victory came with many challenges when we arrived in Canada. We only had five suitcases of belongings for the entire family (my parents and three kids) as we lost all our possessions. In the new country, my parents' diplomas were not acknowledged. In spite of this adversity, they never lost focus or hope, and have achieved many great things which I am tremendously proud of. Their persistence has shaped who I am today and it lives in me and is reflected in every action I take. If I set my mind to achieve something, nothing can or will stand in my way.

> *"Success in most things depends on knowing how long it takes to succeed"* — CHARLES-LOUIS DE SECONDAT, BARON DE LA BRÈDE ET DE MONTESQUIEU (1689-1755)

Perseverance built the pyramids on Egypt's plains, erected the Temple in Jerusalem, and brought to life many of today's inventions and scientific advancements. Perseverance has shaped exquisite creations of genius from marble, and painted on canvas images of nature and people that remain immortalized today. Perseverance has put airplanes in motion when only a few believed we could fly, brought us to the moon, and led to medical breakthroughs that have saved countless lives.

Isaac Newton discovered the law of universal gravitation in his youth, but one slight error in a measurement of the earth's circumference interfered with a demonstration of the correctness of his theory. After twenty years of further work, he corrected the error, and showed that the planets move in their orbits as a result of the same law that brings a falling apple to the ground.

No matter how difficult the circumstances never stop pursuing your goal. Never stop moving forward, evolving and reaching new heights each day. As challenges emerge, look at them in a positive way. Opposing circumstances create strength and power. **Overcoming one barrier gives us greater ability to overcome the next**. In 1492, Columbus, after many years of setbacks, managed to get the support he needed to sail towards the new world. Three days out, his boat floated a signal of distress and terror seized the sailors. But Columbus calmed their fears, and continued moving forward until he reached the "new" world on October 12th.

Montesquieu spent twenty-five years writing his *Esprit des Lois*, and Adam Smith spent ten years on his *Wealth of Nations*. Euripides, one of the last three tragedians of ancient Greece, was known to spend sometimes days in crafting a few lines for his plays. If you look at the people behind the creation of companies such as Ford, Microsoft, Apple, or IBM, perseverance has allowed them to flourish and to introduce and implement innovative ideas when few believed they would ever succeed.

Set your goals clearly, and never give up until you have conquered all obstacles. "*The truest wisdom*," said Napoleon, "*is a resolute determination.*" When the road to success is paved with uncertainties and difficulties, but in the end victory is achieved, this brings the greatest satisfaction.

> *"When you get into a tight place and everything goes against you, till it seems as if you could not hold on a minute longer, never give up then, for that's just the place and time that the tide will turn."*
> – HARRIET BEECHER STOWE (1811-1896)

Great men and women never wait for favorable circumstances to pursue their dreams. They work out their problems, and master the situation, in spite of barriers that may seem insurmountable. Handel composed his great works when he was struck by partial paralysis, but his name remains immortal in music. Mozart composed his great operas, including his "Requiem," while struggling with a fatal disease. Beethoven produced his greatest works when overcome by almost total deafness. Helen Keller became an author, political activist and lecturer although she was deaf and blind.

All that is great and noble in the history of the world is the result of infinitely painstaking effort and persistence. Columbus pursued his cause despite continued rejections from court after court. Rejection did not demolish the purpose which dominated his soul and his desire to explore new lands. You cannot keep determined people from success. Place stumbling-blocks in their way and they take them for stepping-stones on the path to greatness. **Through determination, everything is possible**.

Although willpower is necessary to success, and, other things being equal, the greater the willpower, the grander the success, circumstances and environments also play a role. You must temper determination with knowledge and common sense or it will lead you only to bang your head against the wall. You can do anything within the limit of your utmost faculty, strength, and endurance. Obstacles, as a general rule, are neither insurmountable nor permanent. The strong-willed, intelligent, persistent person will find a way to overcome any challenge. But always remember to **distinguish between factors that you can control and those that you cannot.** In any circumstance, if you get frustrated by the factors you cannot control, you will draw energy away from finding solutions for those you can. While it is true that willpower cannot perform miracles, it is almost omnipotent, and can perform wonders, as history shows. As Shakespeare wrote in *Julius Caesar*:

"Men at some time are masters of their fates;
The fault, dear Brutus, is not in our stars,
But in ourselves, that we are underlings."

Mathematicians say that if you throw two dice, the chances are thirty to one against you turning up a particular number, and a hundred to one against you repeating the same throw three times in succession, and so on. Don't let chance rule your life. There is as much chance that you will achieve success by doing nothing, as there is in producing a great literary work by choosing blindly words from a dictionary and letting your computer put them together randomly. Fortune smiles upon those who roll up their sleeves, focus on their goal and deliver results.

"There is nothing impossible to him who will try" - ALEXANDER THE GREAT (336-323 BC)

"All my work, my life, everything is about survival. All my work is meant to say, - You may encounter many defeats,

but you must not be defeated" – MAYA ANGELOU (1928-)

A few years ago, my husband and I met a great explorer by the name of Michael Horn who had navigated the North Pole on his own. When he was sharing with us the challenges he encountered throughout his journey, we were absolutely amazed by his exploits. He accomplished his goal in spite of the many challenges he faced: he lost all his belongings when his tent caught fire; he suffered from frostbite due to extremely cold temperature; and he endured a Russian prison where he was placed for a couple of months, while waiting for his visa clearance. Whenever I encounter any obstacles, I often recall that meeting and what he said:

"Obstacles are as big as you personally make them" – MICHAEL HORN (1966-)

In other words, we are the creators of the barriers that often stop us from moving forward. Or from another angle, we can create the positive energy required to confront any challenge. According to the National Science Foundation, the average person thinks about 12,000 thoughts per day. If a fraction of these thoughts are negative, imagine how this can influence your actions while you focus on achieving your goal. Transforming a negative thought into a positive one will energize you and give you strength to move forward. By imagining yourself in the future, and visualizing positive rather than negative outcomes, you will be amazed by the power you have to create your future.

Below are a few guiding principles to help you become stronger when facing challenges, and ensure you have the persistence required to reach your goals:

- **Awareness of your goal**: Never lose focus of your goal, in spite of other priorities that may emerge in your life. Do not allow yourself to create excuses for failing to pursue your goal. Carry something with you that reminds you constantly of your goal that you look at several times a day (i.e. customize the wallpaper on your cell phone; carry a card in your wallet with key messages, etc.). The bracelets available through the Successonality Self-Development events are intended for this. Put one on, associate it with your goal, and never conveniently "forget" about your objective.
- **Focus on what YOU can control**: Develop an action plan that includes actions that you can control, rather than those you cannot. Focus on the inter-linkages between your actions, and how they lead to influencing the factors that you may not be able to control. Wasting energy on trying to influence things that you cannot control is futile.
- **Seek support**: Another way for you to stay on track is to become part of a social network and join forces with a group of individuals who are pursuing the same goal as you. This will allow you to share experiences, get inspired by progress made by all individuals in the same network, and feel a sense of belonging to a group that is sharing your priorities. Furthermore, being part of a group creates peer pressure to perform and allows individuals to more easily reach common goals together. You may also seek the advice of a mentor, a coach, your extended circle of friends or partners, since success will more easily be achieved with the proper support.

- **Be creative:** Being creative is key to reaching any goal. You must let your imagination run wild to find new ideas and ways to quickly achieve your goal, or to find innovative ways to solve problems. Step outside your normal routine, take a new route to your house, visit a museum, or read magazines or books that you would not normally read. From my own experience, the more radical the change in my environment, the more creative I become. During my travels I observe and enjoy the aromas of a new place, the change in culture, the architecture and people who inspire me in many different ways. My most creative ideas came to me in foreign lands, when I step outside my routine to experience new things.
- **Be solution-oriented**: As you pursue your action plan, in the face of adversity and obstacles that may come your way, focus on solutions rather than the problem itself until you reach your goal. In times of crisis, you have no time to waste on questioning yourself and on building negative energy. You need to focus on the future, instead of being frustrated about things in the past that can no longer be changed. As a private pilot, I have learned to do this in a fraction of a second. If problems emerge during a flight, I know that I need to take immediate action because every second counts. Going into panic mode will cloud the mind, and will prevent you from finding solutions. You can always reflect on what happened later, in order to learn from the situation and apply the knowledge when the same problem emerges again. However, in the midst of the incident, being solution-oriented will make the difference between success and failure.
- **Believe that failure is not an option**: Every challenge that comes your way can easily become an

excuse for you to stop pursuing your dreams. Whether the challenge will be of a financial nature, a health issue, or a time problem, your natural tendency will be to use it as an excuse to give up. This will allow you to remain within your comfort zone while believing that you had a valid reason for not overcoming the obstacle that forced you to put your dreams on hold. The end result: a life filled with regret. Is this the life you have imagined? Is this what you want to be remembered for? With life being so short, you can no longer make excuses for yourself. You need to believe that **failure is not an option**. When you decide which goals to pursue on the personal or professional level, make a commitment to yourself from the start that you will persist in achieving your goals irrespective of the obstacles that may come your way. You control your destiny, and you control your 12,000 thoughts each day. Force yourself to have two positive thoughts for each negative thought that emerges in your mind. Although discipline will be required in the beginning, this will turn into a habit faster than you think. Be persistent, believe that you will succeed, and you will be marveled by your accomplishments.

"Pain is temporary. Quitting lasts forever." – LANCE ARMSTRONG (1971-)

SELF-CONFIDENCE

Have faith in yourself and expect only great things.

> *"Why should we call ourselves men, unless it be to succeed in everything everywhere?"* – HONORÉ GABRIEL RIQUETI, COMTE DE MIRABEAU (1749-1791)

> *"Self-confidence is the first requisite to great undertakings"* – SAMUEL JOHNSON (1709-1784)

The miracles of civilization have been performed by men and women of great self-confidence, who had unwavering faith in their power to accomplish the tasks they undertook. Our society would be centuries behind where it is today had it not been for their persistence in finding and making real what they believed in and which the world often denounced as impossible.

Nothing should stop you from accomplishing great things and believing in your brilliance. Stay away from people who attempt to destruct your faith in your ability to do the thing you have set your heart on. You will be powerless if you allow your confidence to diminish. Your achievement will never be greater than your self-faith. You cannot achieve anything significant in life if you have doubts and fears about your true ability.

You will achieve success in everything you choose by expecting it, demanding it, assuming it. You must have a strong and firm self-faith first, otherwise nothing will be achieved. Success becomes possible through self-confidence, persistence and boldness. Irrespective of talent, intellectual capacity or education level, the achievement will never rise above the self-confidence. If you think you can achieve something, you will, but, if you think you cannot, you will not. Your beliefs will always influence your future accomplishments.

It does not matter what other people think of you, your plans, or your dreams. No one person or circumstance should discourage you from believing in yourself. Be confident that you will succeed in whatever you set yourself to do and find the strength within you to achieve your highest potential.

Setting low expectations for yourself will not result in accomplishing much. What you become is a reflection of an inward image of yourself. Do not weaken yourself by a mental attitude of self-deprecation. If you do not claim enough, expect enough, or demand enough of yourself, you will not achieve greatness. A vast number of men and women, who are capable of doing great things, do only small things and live mediocre lives because they do not expect or demand enough of themselves. They fail to see that they can control their own destiny and become whatever they envision to be.

You must be self-reliant, optimistic, and pursue your objectives with the assurance of success, and opportunities will emerge in your favor. You will draw to yourself the literal fulfillment of the promise, *"For unto every one that hath shall be given, and he shall have abundance"* (Matthew 25:29). Assume the part you wish to play, and play it royally and think ambitiously.

There is something about the aura of a person who has true self-esteem, a positive attitude and who believes that he or she is going to win no matter what circumstances arise. Confidence begets confidence. Carry yourself with an air of victory, radiate assurance and impart to others confidence that you can achieve everything you attempt. As time goes on, your belief will be reinforced not only by the power of your own thoughts, but also by all who know you. Your friends and acquaintances will affirm and reaffirm your ability to succeed, thus making each successive triumph easier to achieve than its predecessor. Your self-poise, assurance, and confidence will naturally increase as your achievements increase. Every conquest on your journey, whether it is on the personal or professional front, adds to your power to pursue your next big project. **Success today leads to greater success tomorrow**.

Set your mind toward your goal so resolutely, and with such vigorous determination, that nothing on earth can turn you from your purpose until you attain it. This very assertion of superiority, the assumption of power, the affirmation of belief in yourself will strengthen your confidence to a point that doubt and fear will be undermined.

If you doubt your ability to do what you set out to do; if you think that others are better suited to do it than you; if you fear taking chances; if you have more negative thoughts than positive ones; you can never make great progress forward until you change your whole mental attitude and learn to have great faith in yourself. Shift your focus from fear and doubt towards your ambitions, and your role as a great Chief Life Officer with a great life purpose.

Your own mental picture of yourself is a good measure of your ambition and your possibilities. The deed you wish to accomplish must first live in your thoughts and your heart, or it will never be a reality. Having strong and vivid clarity about your dream is a tremendous initial step. A dream that is not well defined cannot be well executed. All the greatest achievements in the world began with a clear dream and desire, even in difficult circumstances. This longing keeps your courage up and makes effort easier until the thing dreamed of is realized.

Your faith in yourself is a very good measure of what you will get out of life. The intensity of your confidence in your ability to do the thing you attempt is related to the degree of your achievement. If we were to analyze the marvelous successes of many self-made men and women, we would find that when they first started out they held a confident, vigorous, and persistent belief in their ability to accomplish what they had undertaken. Their mental attitude was set so stubbornly toward their goal that the doubts and fears that hinder and frighten certain people instead fueled their determination. Thomas Edison had more than 10,000 unsuccessful attempts before he was able to make a revolving piece of wax record and reproduce the sound of the human voice. In spite of this he said, *"I haven't failed. I've found 10,000 ways that don't work."* He met similar challenges before he developed the incandescent electric light bulb. It also took the Wright brothers many attempts before they created the first flying machine. Graham Bell also faced many challenges over several years before the long-distance telephone emerged. Without their self-confidence to continue moving forward in spite of the challenges they faced, we would not have electric light, airplanes or long-distance phones today. Challenges must therefore be looked upon not from a negative perspective, but from a positive angle, given that they bring fresh insight and invaluable knowledge that can help you clear the way forward to reaching your goals.

> *"I am not discouraged, because every wrong attempt discarded is another step forward"* – THOMAS EDISON (1847-1931)

> *"Anyone who has never made a mistake has never tried anything new"* – ALBERT EINSTEIN (1879-1955)

We tend to think of people who have been very successful in any line of endeavor as being greatly favored by fortune, and we try to account for their success in all sorts of ways but the right one. The fact is that their success represents their expectations of themselves, in other words, the sum of their creative, positive, habitual thinking. Their accomplishments reflect their mental attitudes made tangible in their environment. They have created what they have and what they are out of their constructive beliefs and their unwavering faith in themselves.

Believe you can succeed, and believe it with all your heart. There must be vigor in your expectations, in your endeavor and you must have determination that knows no defeat. Concentrate your effort on positive energy to attain your objective. If you cease to believe in yourself and start believing there is a mysterious destiny, out of your control, that influences your life, you have given up. You must believe that you are bigger than any fate, and that you have within yourself a power mightier than any force outside yourself. Do not get held back by too much caution. Do not be timid about venturing into the unknown. Be bold and strong. Whatever you long for, and hold persistently in your mind, you will achieve in proportion to the intensity and persistence of your thoughts. Let go of thoughts of smallness and inferiority. Your mind must be focused firmly toward achievement. You must believe you can achieve success and that you *are* success.

Self-confidence is not egotism. It is knowledge, and it comes from the consciousness of possessing the ability required for what one undertakes. A firm self-faith will help you project yourself with a force that is almost irresistible. There is a great difference between a person who *will try* to do something, and a person who *knows* he/she can do it, who feels bound to do it by an irresistible inner force. The difference between uncertainty and certainty, between vacillation and decision, measures the distance between weakness and power, between mediocrity and excellence, between commonness and superiority.

I once organized a team-building exercise that involved walking on fire. Before we actually did this, we engaged in numerous other exercises, each more difficult than the last. First, we each broke a wooden board with one hand, then we used our necks to first break an arrow and then bend an iron bar. When I first attempted this exercise in Europe, although I was able to break the board and arrow, I struggled to bend the bar. I tried about five times with two different people, until the facilitator asked me to stop before I would hurt myself. My throat was actually sore for over a week and the pain made me think about what had happened.

I realized that I had started this exercise with the belief that "I may be able to do it" and that by trying, I would "know" whether I was capable of it. This hesitation made me doubt in my ability to complete the next exercise, which was to walk on fire. I thought that if I was not able to bend the bar, I would not be able to walk on coals at about 1000 degrees Fahrenheit (550 degrees Celsius). However, walking on fire was the entire "raison d'être" of this team-building, and as the leader of the group, I was obliged to complete the exercise. So I changed my mindset and I succeeded to walk on fire that evening, not only once, but several times.

A few weeks later, I organized the same exercise with my team in North America. This time, I was confident and successful during the workshop because I believed in myself. Rather than saying that "I will try" to complete all the exercises, I said to myself that "I will succeed". The end result: the entire workshop felt effortless, and bending the metal bar did not feel as it was made of iron. This experience has radically changed the way I look at the challenges I undertake. It is at the source of many of the projects I am pursuing today. The facilitator of these two workshops inspired me so much in this process that we became business partners in the Successionality Workshops which we offer globally. Confidence rules, and if doubt creeps upon me once in a while, I think back to this experience and remind myself that I am in full control of my destiny.

The fact that you believe implicitly that you can do what may seem impossible to others shows that there is a force within you that is critical to your success. Self-faith has been the miracle-worker for ages. It has won a thousand triumphs in war, in science, and in business, that were deemed impossible by doubters and the faint-hearted. It has enabled inventors and pioneers to go on amidst troubles and trials, which otherwise would have utterly disheartened them. It has held innumerable scientists to their tasks until their glorious discoveries were accomplished.

By thinking positively and believing in yourself, you can reach superior heights. There is no power in the universe that can help you do a thing that you think you cannot do. Self-faith must lead the way. Believe in your own power, and remember that you cannot go beyond the limits you set for yourself.

You cannot go very far in the world or express great power until you catch a glimpse of your higher, nobler self, and until you realize that your ambition and your aspirations are proofs of your ability to reach the ideal which burns inside you. If you feel the yearning for infinite achievement within you, your ability and the opportunity for realizing it is also within you.

Believe in yourself with all your power. Believe that your destiny is controlled by you. Believe that there is a power within you which, if awakened, developed, and matched with honest effort, will make you successful.

Start believing today, that you are capable of amazing deeds, and engage on the path that will lead you to an extraordinary journey. To achieve this, you must have full control over what you Think, Say and Do:

- **Think**: Your thoughts have to be filled with a strong belief that you can achieve great things, that you are destined for excellence, that you are powerful enough to achieve any goal, and overcome any challenge. Visualize having already achieved your goal, affirm to yourself that you are a fighter, and do not let anyone bring you down. You create your own destiny and the heights of your achievements are correlated with your beliefs. Think big and you will achieve great things.
- **Say**: Replace in your vocabulary "I think I can" with "I can," and "I will try" with "I will achieve." Always be positive, do not complain, and look on the bright side of any situation. Do not forget that challenges are opportunities in disguise.
- **Do**: If you visualize, and say the right things but do not take any action, you will not go very far. Behind every idea, there must be a plan that allows you take a step at a time to reach your goals. Reapply the SMART-P^2 goals discussed in Chapter 1 to build your action plan, stay on track and reach new heights in your life.

EXCELLENCE

Always do your best from the start.

> *"We are what we repeatedly do. Excellence, then, is not an act, but a habit."* – ARISTOTLE (384 BC –322 BC)

> *"Excellence can be attained if you care more than others think is wise. Risk more than others think is safe. Dream more than others think is practical, and expect more than others think is possible."* – ANONYMOUS

Have you ever achieved something remarkable without being diligent about your actions? Diligence implies careful attention to your task to ensure you do things right from the start and consciousness through every step of the way until you achieve your goals. If you do not believe this to be a requirement to success, try to think of someone who has achieved success by being negligent. I doubt you will be able to. Excellence leads to success, while negligence leads to failure. For John Rockefeller, Henry Ford, Thomas Edison, Bill Gates, Oprah Winfrey and Anita Roddick, among other super achievers, demanding excellence was an essential ingredient of their to success. The quality we put into our life-work affects everything else in our lives, and is reflected in our behavior and personality. Your entire being takes on the characteristics of your usual way of doing things. The habit of precision and accuracy strengthens you, and improves your character. Whereas doing things in a careless manner damages your reputation, and demoralizes you.

Excellence is about achieving remarkable things by working intelligently and efficiently. Every mediocre or half-done job you produce diminishes your sense of self-worth. After doing a poor job, you are not quite the same person you were before, and you are not as likely to try to keep up your high standard of work. Introducing inferiority into your work is like introducing subtle poison into your body, and into your life. It dulls ideals, kills ambition, and seriously damages your self-confidence.

Excellence goes hand in hand with honesty. Honesty implies more than always keeping your word; it also implies carefulness, accuracy, and honesty in your work. Any departure from integrity and honesty to your true ideals will demoralize you and taint your whole character. Honesty requires wholeness, thoroughness, and truth in everything, in deed and in word. Never deliver work or services that are tainted by carelessness or indifference, if you want to be regarded as dependable and trustworthy. **You must always give your best in order to be perceived highly by others**. Excellence in what you do brings fulfillment and personal satisfaction because you will have reached your goals, and attained respect and admiration from people who are important to you, whether these be your superiors, your clients or your family.

You will be at peace with yourself when you have the approval of your conscience as a result of pursuing excellence. That will be worth more to you than any amount of money you could pocket through deceitful or careless work. Nothing else can give you the satisfaction and uplift that comes from a superbly done job.

Excellence ultimately influences your reputation. Some of the world's greatest companies have regarded their reputation as their most precious possession, and under no circumstances would they allow their names to be compromised. Companies that have made the *Fortune* or *Forbes* Top lists are constantly reinventing themselves and aiming to achieve excellence in everything they do. At the end of the day, this is reflected in their financial results, the quality of their products and services, and their rating on the stock market.

When you finish any piece of work you must be willing to stand for that piece of work. And you must know deep down that you put your best effort forward to do it as well as you could, to a complete finish, and you must be willing to be judged by it. Never be satisfied with "fairly good" or "good enough." Accept nothing short of your best. Put such quality into your work that anyone who comes across anything you have ever done will see your trademark of superiority upon it. **Your reputation is at stake in everything you do, and your reputation is your capital.** You cannot afford to do a poor job. Every bit of your work, no matter how unimportant or trivial it may seem, should bear your seal of excellence. You should regard every task that you complete as the very best you can do.

It is the seemingly small difference between the "good" and the "best" that makes the difference between leaders and followers, winners and losers. The little touches beyond what an average person may deliver can make a difference in your fame. Regard your work as Stradivari regarded his violins, which he "made for eternity" and of which not one was ever known to break. Stradivari did not need any patent on his violins, for no other violin maker matched his level of excellence or took such pains to put the stamp of superiority upon his instruments. Every "Stradivarius" now in existence, over 300 years later, is hailed for its superlative tonal quality and superior craftsmanship. In recent auctions, the Stradivari violins were sold for over USD 3.5 million, the most paid to date for any musical instrument.

John D. Rockefeller, Jr. said that the "*secret of success is to do the common duty uncommonly well.*" **The thing you are doing today will either unlock or bar the door to**

advancement in the future. Your everyday actions that are in line with reaching your vision must be done diligently. If you demand the best and will accept nothing less, if you insist on keeping up your standards in everything you do, you will achieve distinction in your line of work. But if you are satisfied with "good enough" work, and are not particular about the quality of your work or your personal habits, then you cannot expect to accomplish great things with your life.

Those who have achieved success have never been satisfied to do things just as others do them, but have always insisted on doing them a little better. It is the constant effort to be first-class in everything one attempts that conquers the heights of excellence. When it comes to new inventions, excellence and attention to every single detail can make the difference between a product that will become a market leader vs. one that simply exists. A family friend who was an engineer, had done this so brilliantly that he made a fortune out of patented inventions, from buttonhole machines to car reflectors, to name a few.

Make it a life rule to give your best to whatever passes through your hands. Let superiority be your trademark, let it characterize everything you touch. This is what you should strive for whether you are self-employed or working for a company. Never allow yourself to dwell too much upon what you are getting for your work in terms of compensation. You have something of infinitely greater value at stake. Your honor, your whole career, your future success, will be affected by the way you do your work.

If you are learning a new trade or doing something new, and are unable to fully judge your work, seek advice from people you trust about the quality of your work. Even though receiving harsh criticism may be difficult, you will soon realize this advice will allow you to improve your skills to reach new heights faster. Always seek advice from the best, from people you admire and aspire to be like.

If any work you do is skimped or botched, your character will suffer. If your work is badly done, if it falls to pieces, if there is inferior workmanship in it, your character will suffer. Behind some of the largest product recalls by huge corporations, which in certain cases have caused death or injury to consumers, there was a person or group of people who simply did not do their job well enough, overlooked important details, and ignored the consequences of their actions. These individuals and the corporation's reputation can be forever tarnished, and the damage caused is often irreversible.

We are so constituted that every deviation from what is right causes loss of self-respect and makes us unhappy. Every time we do right, we hear an inward approval and every time we fail to, a protest or condemnation. Whatever your vocation, let quality always prevail in everything you do. And never forget the consequences of your work on others. Don't think you will never hear about a half-finished job, a neglected or low-quality piece of work. It will show up farther along in your career at the most unexpected moment, in the most embarrassing situation. It will mortify you when you least expect it.

How do you measure the quality of what you do? One way is known as 360 degrees feedback. This consists in receiving anonymous feedback on your performance, from staff, peers, clients, suppliers, partners and other stakeholders with whom you interact frequently. I suggest applying this to any circumstance when you would like to get the pulse on how you are doing. First, you must seek advice from the best people around you as a priority, in order to gain insights from a trained eye. Second, there are three questions you must ask yourself and others you trust to improve your skills and evaluate your overall performance:

- **What am I doing well that I should CONTINUE doing?** I suggest rating your performance on a scale from 1 to 3 (1 for good, 2 for very good, and 3 for excellent). This will allow you to prioritize the areas where you require more effort to reach excellence. Seek opinions from several people about your performance, and select individuals who can truly provide feedback on your work.
- **What am I not doing well that I should IMPROVE on?** We all have areas to improve on, so be prepared to receive negative feedback as part of your learning curve. Although it may be difficult to accept, it will help you improve beyond measure.
- **What should I STOP doing?** This question may be very difficult to ask, but it will benefit you tremendously. You must seek clarification about why you must stop doing the specific action that is preventing you from reaching your goal.

By thinking in terms of *Continue, Improve and Stop*, these questions will more easily be remembered. However, when receiving feedback on what you should improve and stop doing, be prepared to go through what is called the *Kübler-Ross grief cycle* (Kübler-Ross Elisabeth, *On Death and Dying*, 1973, Routledge). This is a natural process that many people go through when grieving; it has been adapted by business psychologists to apply to situations in which negative input is received. The stages of the cycle are described below:

1. **Shock**: Many people will be taken by surprise by the true facts of their performance as they are perceived by others. This period can last a

few hours to a few days, depending on the person and circumstances.
2. **Denial:** Certain individuals will not believe that the negative feedback is legitimate, and will refuse to recognize or acknowledge the input received. Being in denial can also last a few hours to a few days, depending on the severity of the feedback received.
3. **Anger:** This is the stage often filled with emotional outbursts and frustrations, although different people express varying degrees of anger. Some people may internalize this anger, especially if they are introverts by nature, while others may externalize it more openly. Who said that getting bad news or feedback would be easy?
4. **Acceptance**: At this stage, people begin accepting the feedback received, and look at it as an opportunity to advance and improve.
5. **Action**: People in this stage are now ready to take action in order to improve on the areas they are not performing well in, and to build the foundations for a brighter future.

Whatever you do, be open to criticism and review your performance regularly by using the 360 degree feedback method or other methods that you prefer. As you advance in your career, you will come to realize that expectations increase as your responsibilities increase. Look at this fact as an opportunity to grow, to perfect your skills, and to make the continuous desire for excellence your goal. Turn your life work into a masterpiece that you and the generations to come will be proud of.

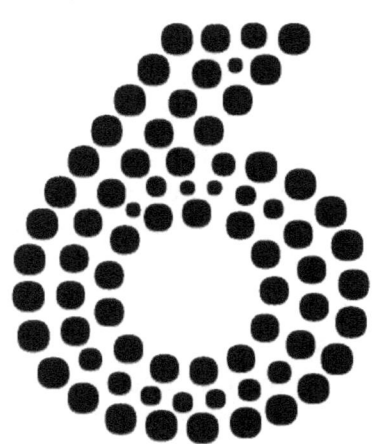

DARE

Live with no fear, live with no regrets.

"Life shrinks or expands in proportion to one's courage" - ANAÏS NIN (1903-1977)

"No great deed is done by falterers who ask for certainty" - GEORGE ELIOT (1819-1880)

"Do not anticipate trouble, or worry about what may never happen. Keep in the sunlight" – BENJAMIN FRANKLIN (1706-1790)

Fear paralyzes people from moving toward their dreams and destroys one's self-confidence. Instead of seeing the positive side of things, fear leads people to imagine dark outcomes, which can lead to an extreme sense of anxiety or distress. Once fear invades a life to this degree, it can become debilitating. We unfortunately have the potential for immense negative mental power over ourselves whether the threat is real or imagined. John Locke, a seventeenth-century English philosopher, said it best: *"Fear is an uneasiness of the mind, upon the thought of future evil likely to befall us."* In reality the future will always be unknown, and this can either make life frightening or exciting, depending on how you choose to look at things. A wonderful friend and business partner of mine, Nancy Chernoff, likes to say that **FEAR** is "**F**alse **E**vidence **A**ppearing **R**eal." Do not let things that are not real stop you from pursuing a dream. Focus on constructive energy rather than a destructive one. Shift your mind from the negative to the positive, and find the force within you to believe that you can overcome any challenge.

Don't waste time dreaming of obstacles you may never encounter or crossing bridges you have not reached. Live with no fear if you want to live with no regrets. Thoughts are but dreams until you begin taking action. Find the energy to take the first step to overcome your fears by doing one thing that you are afraid of every day. Whether it is public speaking or defending something you believe in, you need to start taking small steps each day. By doing this, you will build your confidence to pursue greater challenges.

A few years ago, my husband and I decided to take flying lessons. He had been flying in Europe since he was sixteen, and now wanted to get his pilot license in Canada. When I decided to get mine as well, I felt more fear than pleasure. I simply wanted to pilot a plane to assist my husband in case of an emergency. My desire to become a private pilot was driven by fear for his safety. However, after the first few flights, I became addicted to it and flying became my true passion. I realized that the slightest error while flying could have fatal consequences; therefore, I knew I had to remain mentally and physically sharp in order to fly. I no longer call this the fear factor, but rather the reality factor. Flying for me is now about freedom, discovery, and pleasure.

When you look back in history, it is astonishing to see what courage and perseverance have enabled many individuals to achieve. Alexander the Great, who ascended the throne at twenty, was one of the most successful commanders of all times, and had conquered the known world before dying at thirty-three. Julius Caesar captured eight hundred cities, conquered three hundred nations, defeated three million men, and became a renowned orator and one of the greatest statesmen known. Joan of Arc led the French army to several important victories during the Hundred Years' War in her teens. Marie Curie was a pioneer in the field of radioactivity and won two Nobel Prizes for her contributions to science.

There are also many examples of companies that started in recession periods and overcame the fears that were prevalent during the difficult economic times. Microsoft, FedEx, LexisNexis all started their operations in the early seventies, in the midst of an oil crisis and an economic downturn. Burger King and Hyatt were created during the 1957-58 recession, and GE (General Electric) was founded in 1876 by Thomas Edison in the midst of a multi-year recession. Their founders recognized that there was a market need and filled it, and overcame all possible fears that emerged linked to launching a company during an economic slowdown. Taking calculated risks during these times led them to turn their dreams into internationally renowned companies.

Whatever people may think, always do what you believe to be right. If you continuously get diverted and influenced by the fears of negative individuals, stop associating yourself with them. Be indifferent to censure, and stay on course. Always remember that **your success depends on you, and only you**. As Henry Ford said:

> *"If you say you can, you can;*
> *If you say you can't, you can't;*
> *They are both right."*

The brave person is not the one who feels no fear, but the one who manages to subdue fear and bravely dares the danger others shrink from. The biggest risk in life isn't making mistakes, but regret. Below are a few guiding principles that can assist you in breaking the wall of fear that is stopping you from moving forward:

1. **Identify your fear**: There are multiple types of fears that stand in our way of advancement that vary from person to person. Are you afraid of losing your health, your assets, your loved ones, or of being criticized? These are in line with the *Maslow's Hierarchy of Needs Theory* which states that the highest human need is self-actualization, in other words, the desire to become the best you can be. Self-actualization is at the top of the pyramid and is followed by esteem, love/belonging, safety/health and psychological needs (food, water, oxygen, etc.). However, you cannot attend to your highest needs until you have attended to those at the bottom of the pyramid, which revolve around **health, wealth** and **love**. If you fear that your basic needs are threatened, or that you could lose your health by pursuing a new venture, or lose the wealth you have accumulated by starting a new business and hence be criticized by family members and friends, this fear will stop you from moving forward. Before you move to step 2, you need to identify all the fears that are stopping you today from pursuing your dreams and from becoming a great Chief Life Officer. Write these fears on paper for each one of your key goals, and do not be afraid of having a long list. Success in the following phases will depend on the sincerity of your list.

2. **Analyze your fear**: When looking at fear, we often look only at possible negative outcomes, and often forget the positive results and benefits from overcoming a specific fear. Take the list of all your fears and create two columns next to it, one labeled "worst case scenario" and another "best case

scenario." First, begin reflecting on the worst possible scenario that may emerge if you do decide to move forward with your plans, and write your ideas down by marking each Problem with a P. For each one of the "worst case scenarios," write all possible solutions that you could take to deal with the circumstances: under each Problem, write S for Solution and specify what you will do to overcome each Problem. In the "best case scenario" column, begin enumerating the positive outcomes that may emerge if your fear does not materialize. Once this exercise is complete, you should have your roadmap for viable solutions that you can pursue in case challenges emerge on your journey towards your dreams. This should give you the confidence that there is always a solution to any problem.

3. **Overcome your fear**: Start building an action plan for your project with specific time frames, and built-in weekly reviews that allow you to evaluate progress and realign your actions. You also need to build in "go/no-go" decision points once you have reached key milestones. In order to make the choice to pursue the project forward (a "go" decision), you need to reach certain pre-established conditions that you can define, and that are within your comfort zone. If these conditions do not materialize, you can then decide to stop moving the project forward (a "no-go" decision) for an interim period, or permanently. You can decide the level of risk you are willing to take every step of the way, depending on the level of success you are achieving. For example, if you would like to start your own business and you require an investment that would tap into your savings, you may choose to move forward more slowly in the beginning. Instead of taking out 100% of your savings, start at 15%, and go

as high as 50% if certain profit levels are reached within a certain period of time; this would be a pre-established condition that will trigger your go/no-go decision. With the profits you will generate from your first investment, you can continue the growth path of your company, rather than continue tapping into your personal savings. Therefore, the fear of losing your money will diminish if you plan things smartly. Furthermore, you need to take timing into consideration. We all have different appetites for risk that we can endure before the stress levels could lead to health problems. Only you know what is endurable for you. Take this into consideration as you build your action plan.

Action will always cure your fears. However, you must take **calculated or intelligent risks** at every phase of your progress to truly be successful. Taking calculated risks implies that you are not overlooking critical details that could make a difference between success and failure. In the early phases of your project, ask yourself the following questions when you are struggling to decide if you are heading in the right direction:

- Assuming you have done a thorough evaluation of the potential gains/benefits of an action, are the potential gains from taking a specific risk worth the personal and financial investment (in terms of time, energy and money)?
- If your success is predominately conditional on things out of your control, do you have a solid and realistic plan that you think can influence indirectly the uncontrollable factors and stakeholders, in order for you to be successful?

- Do you have a clear understanding of the real risks associated with your actions, of the unforeseen obstacles that may emerge, their probability of arising and do you have a clear risk mitigation plan in place?

If you have answered "yes" to all the above questions, you are on the right track and are truly taking calculated risks. If you have answered "no" to at least one of the questions, rethink your strategies, and re-evaluate your risks. Taking calculated risks is crucial to your survival and your success.

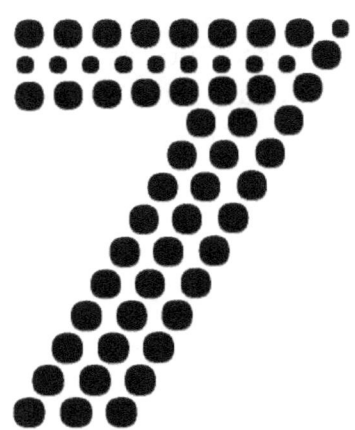

SEIZE THE MOMENT

Don't let opportunities pass you by.

"The secret of success in life is for a man to be ready for his opportunity when it comes" - BENJAMIN DISRAELI (1802-1881)

"Small opportunities are often the beginning of great enterprises" - DEMOSTHENES (384-322 BC)

"You must live in the present, launch yourself on every wave, find your eternity in every moment. Fools stand on their island of opportunities and look towards another land. There is no other land; there is no other life but this." – HENRY DAVID THOREAU (1817-1862)

Opportunities! Every life is full of them. The *"Acres of Diamonds"* story told by Russell Conwell in his motivational speeches around the world conveys eloquently how we often don't need to look far to find opportunities.

The story (as described in *Acres of Diamonds: -1915*, Russell Herman Conwell, Cornell University Press, 2009) is about a Persian man by the name of Ali Hafed who had everything one could wish for—a house on the river, a wife, children, an extensive farm, gardens filled with flowers, orchards loaded with fruit, and miles of forest. He was content and happy. One evening a priest visited him and explained to him how the world was made—how the first beams of sunlight condensed on the earth's surface into a diamond mine—and told him that if the mine was found, there would be enough diamonds to buy many farms like his and even a kingdom. After hearing the story, Ali Hafed no longer felt like a rich man and decided to go on a global quest for the diamond mine. He sold the farm for what he could get, left his family, took the money he had, and went in search of the coveted treasure. He wandered for years, but found no diamonds. When his money was all gone, poor Ali Hafed threw himself into the ocean and drowned. The man who bought his farm made the most of his surroundings, and did not believe in going away from home to hunt for diamonds or success. While his camel was drinking in the garden one day, he noticed a flash of light from the white sands of a stream of water. What originally looked like a pebble was in fact a diamond from the legendary mine. Had Ali Hafed been content to remain at home and dig in his own garden instead of going abroad in search of wealth, he would have been a very rich man. The lesson: don't look too far, since opportunities are all around you.

Open eyes will discover opportunities that closed ones will not notice, open ears will hear a story or a conversation that can lead to opening new doors, and open hearts will cherish all circumstances as a blessing. Innumerable apples had fallen from trees before Sir Isaac Newton reasoned that apples fall to earth according to the same law that holds the planets in their orbits, from which he developed his *Theory of Gravitation*. Fortune will come to smile upon all of us, but if we are not ready to receive this gift, it will go in the front door and out the window.

History provides many examples of men and women who have seized occasions to accomplish things deemed impossible by less resolute minds. Prompt decision-making and action are key to success. **Don't wait for extraordinary opportunities. Seize common occasions and make them extraordinary.** As Thomas Edison said, *"Opportunity is* *missed by most people since it is dressed in overalls and it looks like work."*

John D. Rockefeller saw his opportunity in petroleum. He partnered with Samuel Andrews and started with a single barrel in 1870. They made superior-grade oil and prospered rapidly. Not too long after a third partner, Mr. Flagler, joined them, Andrews became dissatisfied. When Rockefeller asked him how much he wanted for his shares, Andrews requested one million dollars. Shortly after, Mr. Rockefeller handed him the requested amount, and they parted ways. At the time, Andrews didn't recognize the true potential in the opportunity they were pursuing. After twenty years in business, the little refinery, worth scarcely a few thousand dollars in the beginning, had grown into the Standard Oil Trust, worth a fortune. Opportunities often take time to flourish. Giving up, or pulling away too fast may deprive you of phenomenal success later on. Timing and patience must be carefully weighed.

Rockefeller was one among many who saw opportunities during the 1860s and 1870s, a time when the American economy changed tremendously. J.P. Morgan, Andrew Carnegie, George Baker and James Graham Fair also saw the huge potential in various areas during that time, and pursued these opportunities, improved on them and worked hard to achieve success. They acted with speed in seizing what they recognized as opportunities, and became millionaires through action and persistence. If an opportunity knocks on your door, seize it then, at the hour when fortune smiles, before it disappears into the sunset.

Opportunities? They are all around us. There are ideas lying latent everywhere, waiting for the observant eye to discover them. Michelangelo transformed a piece of discarded Carrara marble into his statue of David, which has been admired by millions of people over the years. J.K. Rowling came up with the idea for the Harry Potter books while she was on a four-hour-delayed train from Manchester to London. Her books have been translated into 65 languages and have set records as the fastest-selling books in history, and Rowling is now a billionaire. Many of us miss great opportunities in life by waiting to find the perfect ingredients for our creations, when they really lie hidden in the common things around us that we take for granted. One person may go through life without seeing any chances for doing something great, while another close by may draw opportunities for achieving amazing results from the same circumstances. You can make your life sublime by seizing on common occasions and making them great, and maybe you too will make great discoveries like Newton, Faraday and Edison, or paint immortal pictures like Michelangelo or Raphael. Golden opportunities are never offered twice. Seize the moment.

> *"Nature, when she adds difficulties, adds brains"* – RALPH WALDO EMERSON (1803-1882)

> *"Success is to be measured not so much by the position that one has reached in life as by the obstacles which he has overcome"* – BOOKER T. WASHINGTON (1856-1915)

Even challenges and obstacles should be looked at as opportunities in disguise. Two of the greatest epic poets of the world, Homer and Milton, were blind. In spite of these physical challenges, these great creators produced works of art which are masterpieces. In the sciences, Stephen Hawkings' neuromuscular dystrophy did not stop him from producing the bestseller *A Brief History of Time*, which stayed on the British *Sunday Times* bestseller list for 237 weeks.

Failure often leads to success by arousing latent energy, by firing up a dormant purpose, and by awakening powers within you. People with courage turn disappointments into victories just as the oyster turns sand trapped in its shell into a pearl.

> *"Little minds are tamed and subdued by misfortunes; but great minds rise above them"* - WASHINGTON IRVING (1783-1859)

Donald Trump lost millions, before he rose up again to regain his billionaire status. Journalist Tyler Brule started working on creating a new magazine while he was hospitalized after having been shot in Afghanistan. He launched *Wallpaper* magazine in 1996 as a result of this effort, and sold it a few years later to *Time Warner*.

Below are a few guidelines to help you seize each moment and each opportunity:

- **Become like a magnet**: Open your eyes and believe that you can attract opportunities your way. An article or a book you may read, a speech at a conference, or an informal discussion with a friend may lead to potential opportunities, or solutions to problems you may be faced with. If you open your mind and absorb new insights, and create new connections as you are exposed to new ideas, opportunities will emerge. Believe in serendipity, and that you can draw your way the right people

and circumstances when you most need them, even when you are looking for something else entirely.
- **Turn challenges into opportunities**: Challenges and obstacles need to be looked upon as opportunities in disguise. When faced with a challenge, ask yourself "What is this experience teaching me?" and "How can I make the best of the situation I am in?" Focus on sources of constructive energy and positive thoughts that catalyze you forward, instead of destructive energy that brings you down and makes your situation seem worse than it is. Dr. Max Huber did this remarkably well. While an aerospace physicist with NASA, he suffered a horrific accident during a routine experiment which left him with severe burns on his face. Faced with no solutions on the market, he decided to develop his own skin cream. After twelve years and thousands of experiments, he created a miracle cream named *La Mer* which improved his condition and is now owned by Estée Lauder.
- **Validate**: Before making a decision about whether or not to pursue the opportunity in front of you, you must distinguish between **facts** and **opinions**. Facts are based on concrete measurable data available from reliable sources, while opinions are fostered by personal beliefs. Make sure you are thinking critically rather than emotionally as you look at the opportunity in front of you.
- **Trust your instincts**: You can make decisions with your head, your heart, or your instinct. In cases where you do not have enough facts to make a decision about a specific opportunity, you have to trust your instincts about whether or not to pursue it. A great example of trusting instincts comes from the company 3M. Although 3M created the "glue that did not stick" in 1968, it was only in 1980 that

the company launched Post-It notes. The original inventor of the glue was thinking with his head only and was being critical of what he had produced. A few years later, a different 3M employee started thinking with his instinct, and became creative about converting the glue that did not stick into a product that now generates billions of dollars in sales. Remember that **you cannot think critically and creatively at the same time.** When faced with a challenging situation, force yourself to separate the way you look at finding solutions by doing a critical analysis first, followed by a creative analysis.

- **Speed of action**: When faced with a true opportunity, time is of the essence. If you do not pursue a golden opportunity, someone else will. And in many cases, first mover advantage will determine future success. In fact, studies have found that in the corporate world, the first three entrants into the market with a new innovative product or service have higher profit margins than late entrants, who often do not earn enough to repay their investment in development (*Fast Innovation*, by Michael George, James Works, Kimberly Watson-Hemphill, McGraw-Hill, 2005). Quick decision making ability is a sign of leadership and is a must if one is to fully take advantage of future opportunities and become a great Chief Life Officer.

- **Networking:** Expand your network and stay in contact with people who you meet in diverse circumstances, from professional associations to leisure activities. You never know when an innocent encounter might lead to something great in the future. A few years ago, I met a surgeon while taking a glass-making course. A few months later, my father was diagnosed with cancer and required immediate surgery. My contact turned out to be the best surgeon in the city specializing in my father's condition. With the surgeon's help, arrangements for my father's operation were made within days, ultimately saving my father's life. Never underestimate chance encounters, because you never know what door they may open for you in the future.

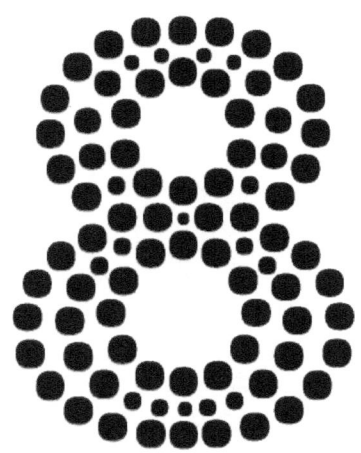

CREATIVITY & PASSION

Find creative solutions. Pursue your passion.

"Nothing great in the world has ever been accomplished without passion" – GEORG WILHELM FRIEDRICH HEGEL (1770-1831)

"Imagination is more important than knowledge" – ALBERT EINSTEIN (1879-1955)

"Creativity is not in the finding of a thing, but the making something out of it after it is found" – JAMES RUSSELL LOWELL (1819-1891)

Creativity is a key ingredient for success. No matter how grand your vision or how strong your persistence, innovation will distinguish your ability to find solutions and pursue opportunities that will allow your brilliance to stand out. When you look at those who are phenomenally successful today, you realize that creativity was the key ingredient for their accomplishments. They looked at current issues or existing products and adapted them ingeniously in order to bring greater value. There are many current examples, such as the evolution of the traditional roller skates into roller blades, or the creation of the Wii by Nintendo, which revolutionized the game industry by introducing consoles that recognize body movements. From the creation of airplanes and phones, to electrical devices and computers—behind all the great inventions that have changed the way we live today—lay creativity, passion and persistence. The world is in constant evolution leading to change and discoveries, and creating many new opportunities.

All great works of art and inventions have been produced when the artists or creators were intoxicated with a passion for beauty or progress that would not let them rest until their thoughts were expressed in the real world. As Yoshihisa Tabuchi said, *"innovation comes from creative destruction"*; often the most miraculous innovations have emerged as a result of great innovators tearing down obsolete views and looking at the world with new eyes. Evolution is about renewal and change, and creativity is a core part of this process.

It is the passion and creativity of great women and men that make our world a better place, where remedies for disease are found, and new discoveries open a new world of endless possibilities. These great women and men create miracles and beauty through their passion, from Steve Jobs, who revolutionized Apple by delivering sleek new designs for his products that outpaced the competition, to Jeff Bezos of Amazon who created the Kindle, an electronic device that allows books to be read electronically. Solar Impulse is another great example of creativity and passion. Since the end of 2003, Bertrand Piccard and André Borschberg have been on a journey to develop an airplane propelled solely by solar energy, without fuel or polluting emissions, which will fly day and night. This dream became a reality in 2010 when they did their first flight tests. Their pioneering work will likely be the foundation for the way planes will be made in the next few decades.

People of passion and enthusiasm see no darkness ahead; they forget that there is such a thing as failure in the world. Many people seem to think that ambition is a quality born within us, that it is not susceptible to improvement, that it is something thrust upon us which will flourish by itself. But the passion that fuels ambition responds very quickly to cultivation and requires constant care and education, just as the faculty for music or art does, or it will atrophy.

If you pursue what you love and what you are passionate about, you are closer to success than you think. By following your passion, not only will you be more energized, but you will also be more creative. Without passion, it is difficult to find the energy and enthusiasm to pursue grand projects in your life, and to overcome the fears that may emerge on your journey.

Passion and creativity can be aroused in anyone, as if from a long sleep, by reading an inspiring book, by listening to a stimulating lecture, or by meeting a supportive friend, someone who understood and encouraged you in the past. It will make all the difference in the world whether you are with people who believe in you, encourage and praise you, or are with those who are forever breaking your confidence, destroying your hopes and criticizing your aspirations. These people destroy your ability to be creative.

Even the strongest of us are not beyond the reach of our environment. No matter how independent, strong-willed and determined our nature, we are constantly being influenced by our surroundings. It does not take much to determine the lives of most of us. We naturally follow the examples around us, and generally, we rise or fall according to the strongest current in which we live. Everything in your past life, every lecture or conversation you have heard, every person who has touched your life, has left an imprint upon your character.

Whatever you do in life, make the necessary sacrifice to keep in an ambition-arousing atmosphere, an environment that will stimulate you to self-development and creativity. Keep close to people who understand you, who believe in you, who will encourage you to make the most of yourself and pursue your passion. This may make all the difference between becoming a grand success and leading a mediocre existence. Stick close to those who are trying to do something and to be somebody in the world, people with high aims and great ambition. Keep close to those who are successful. **Ambition and creativity are contagious.** The success of those around you who are trying to climb upward will encourage and stimulate you reach your dreams.

Life is all about creation, since everyday you create your own success blueprint for the future. Creation is fuelled by passion and enthusiasm, and others can often feel this passion when someone is on a path to greatness. There is great power in a group of individuals who are focused on achieving high aims, a strong magnetic force which will help you attract the object of your ambition. It is very stimulating to be with people whose aspirations run parallel with your own. If you lack energy, if you are naturally lazy or inclined to take it easy, you will be urged forward by the constant encouragement of the more ambitious.

Below are a few tips for bringing more creativity and passion into your life:

- **Find, leverage and enhance your strengths**: Find your strengths and leverage them to pursue your passion. Think about specific tasks or activities that you perform almost effortlessly, the ones that energize and motivate you. We all have things we are particularly good at and that we love to do, and things we hate to do. List the things you love to do, and begin reflecting on how your passions and strengths can be enhanced and leveraged more frequently to pursue your dreams.

- **Diversity**: Staying within your comfort zone, doing things the same way over and over, will kill your imagination. Change your route to the grocery store or your office, or turn your coffee break into a walking break. These small changes have proven successful in changing brain patterns, and can help you be more creative in the long term. The best ideas often emerge when you take a step back from a problem you are trying to tackle, when you engage in an activity that is radically different, and all of a sudden a solution or inspiration may emerge. Going for a walk in the park, going to a museum, exercising or listening to inspirational music can bring surprising results if you open your heart to receive inspiration from the universe. Interactions with people of diverse ages, professions and interests can also be catalysts for creativity, since these people will bring fresh perspectives that you may have not thought of. The more diverse the group of individuals you interact with, the wilder the ideas that will emerge. As different ideas are considered and you start to connect information received from various sources, all the pieces of the puzzle will begin to fit into place. This is where your true creativity will emerge.
- **Change the way you look at everything around you**: Many new inventions came about as a result of inspirations in other industries or sectors that were tackling a similar challenge. The creative person is always accumulating knowledge by not merely looking with the eyes, but by truly seeing with them. The majority of people do not *see* things, they just *look* at them. The power of keen observation is indicative of a superior mentality, since it is the mind (and not the optic nerve) that really sees.

Inspiration can come from anywhere — you just need to open your eyes, and your mind, to see.
- **Positive social context**: Choose your entourage well since your friends influence you more than you think. Think about how you feel when you meet someone who is positive and energized, versus someone who is depressed and negative. Energy is contagious and will influence you subconsciously. Always ensure that you stay in an ambition-arousing and positive environment that will stimulate your creativity. Surround yourself with people who will encourage you to pursue your passion, and who respect and encourage your creative side.
- **Play**: The famous Swiss psychiatrist Carl Jung said that *"the creation of something is not accomplished by the intellect, but by the play instinct acting from inner necessity. The creative mind plays with objects it loves."* Engaging in playful activities can allow you to unwind, relax and enjoy life more, and ultimately be more creative. Think back to when you were a child and to the activities that sparked your creativity, or look at children around you for inspiration. For children, through play, creativity rules. They dream, they fantasize, they have fun and they sometimes come up with the wildest ideas. Become more playful, daydream, dance, sing, laugh more, and do whatever you consider fun each day. Life that allows room for play will always be more creative and fun.
- **Go from creation to realization:** Imagination and creativity without action are worthless. As Thomas Edison said, *"The value of an idea lies in using it."* No matter how wild and crazy your idea may appear, take action to give it life. Einstein knew that no idea

could be too far-fetched. He used to say, "*If at first the idea is not absurd, then there is no hope for it.*"

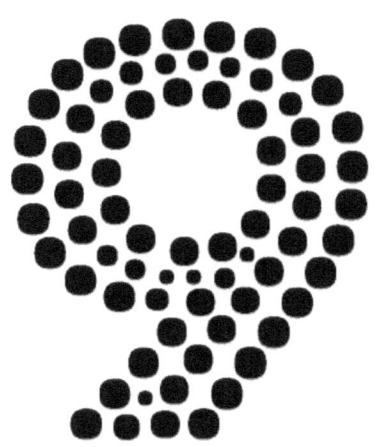

SELF DEVELOPMENT

Expand your knowledge daily.

"The aim of life is self-development. To realize one's nature perfectly, that is what each of us is here for." — OSCAR WILDE (1854–1900)

"Be not afraid of growing slowly, be only afraid of standing still" — CHINESE PROVERB

"There is only one good, knowledge. And one evil, ignorance." — SOCRATES (469-399 BC)

Charles Darwin, Jackson Pollock, Marcel Proust, M.C. Escher, Ray Charles, and Paul Cézanne were all considered by many to have little potential in their early days. How is it possible that these great figures evolved to astonishing heights that brought them world recognition? According to Carol Dweck, it is a matter of *"Mindset,"* as she titled her book on the subject (*Mindset: The New Psychology of Success*, by Carol Dweck, Ballantine Books, 2007). In it, she argues that certain individuals have a "growth mindset" and know that the capacity to develop a certain skill can take time, and thrive on seeking challenges and on constantly stretching themselves. At the opposite end of the spectrum, people with a "fixed mindset" are afraid of challenges, do not believe in pushing themselves, and expect to attain effortless success. The growth-mindset individuals do not look at defeats as failures, but rather as opportunities for learning. As Carol Dweck points out, "when people believe their basic qualities can be developed, failures may still hurt, but failures don't define them. And if abilities can be expanded — if change and growth are possible — then there still may be many paths to success." If you are open to growth and curiosity, and you desire to expand your skills, then you have a "growth mindset." Will the journey be easy? Not necessarily.

Self-improvement implies one essential feeling — the desire to improve one's skills, cultural awareness, and knowledge. If the desire for self-improvement burns in you, the opportunities are endless. In this day of limitless sources of information, from the Internet to libraries, there is no good excuse to neglect growth and development. Irrespective of your education level, **do not create limitations in terms of how much you can learn and grow.** If education has been neglected in your past, either because of lack of opportunity or because you did not take advantage of the opportunities that came your way, self-improvement is still possible as long as you are committed to growth. All skills are learnable, but to truly grow, learning must become a constant practice. You must create a habit of knowledge and skill acquisition that lives in you every day. You must be well read and stay in tune with the latest developments that interest you, while at the same time diversifying your knowledge acquisition. This can be achieved by reading, taking new courses or seminars, taking on new projects and connecting with people who share common interests or are experts in a specific field. You may learn much more from a fifteen-minute discussion with a recognized expert in a specific field than from reading many books. Tangible experience is also a must for expanding your knowledge base. What you live through and experience hands-on marks you in different ways than those things you learn through theoretical information. If you want to expand your painting or photography skills, once you have learned the techniques, you must take your camera or canvas out and begin experimenting, to continue learning and reinforcing your acquired skills. As Einstein used to say *"the only source of knowledge is experience."*

If you have ever been surprised to find yourself falling behind your competitors, start examining yourself. You will likely find that you have stopped growing because you have ceased your effort to keep abreast of the latest developments in your line of work, to read widely and to enrich your life with culture. Try to leverage spare moments to read and study since doing so may open new avenues in the future. People who are willing to make present sacrifices for future gain are the ones who have a higher probability of success in the future. They have the "growth mindset." Self-improvement takes effort and determination, but it will pay off in the end. If you have the disposition for self-improvement and advancement, you will find the opportunity to rise or create new opportunities. One of the sad things about neglected opportunities for self-improvement is that they put people of great natural ability at a disadvantage. There are no bitterer regrets than those that come from letting opportunities pass by.

The biblical parable of the talents illustrates and enforces one of nature's laws: "*To him that hath shall be given; from him that hath not shall be taken away even that which he hath*" (Mark 4:25, Matthew 13:12). Nature is liberal with us if we make the most what she gives us, but if we stop using it, if we do not transform what she gives us into power, if we do not build something, we not only find the supply cut off, but we find that we grow weaker, less efficient. Everything in nature is on the move, either one way or the other. It is either going up or down. It is either advancing or retrograding. Nature withdraws muscle and brain cells if we do not use them. She withdraws skill the moment we stop using our power. Force is withdrawn when we cease exercising it. You need to look at your mind as if it were a muscle. Your effort in building your muscles is directly proportional to your effort. The more you work on building them, the more your strength will grow. When you stop exercising, your muscle tone and strength will diminish. The same goes for the mind. Constant knowledge acquisition and an active and curious mind will ensure you stay sharp mentally, allowing you to look at opportunities with new eyes and to deal with problems that come your way more quickly and more creatively. Knowledge is power and this power will contribute to your success, depending on whether you choose to use this knowledge to your advantage.

One hour a day withdrawn from your normal pursuits and profitably leveraged would enable you to master a complete science. One hour a day would, in ten years, make an ignorant person a well-informed person. An hour a day of reading would allow you to read several books per year. An hour a day might make all the difference between bare existence and productive, successful living. An hour a day might make an unknown man or woman a famous one. Consider, then, the possibilities lost in two, four, or more hours a day used unwisely, for example watching endless hours of television or Internet surfing without a specific purpose. Every person should have a hobby to occupy the leisure hours, something useful to which he or she can turn with delight. If you choose wisely, the study, research and occupation that a hobby confers, it will broaden your character and expand your skills in the areas you are most passionate about.

Great men and women have rarely wasted spare moments. Cicero said: "*What others give to public shows and entertainments, even to mental and bodily rest, I give to the study of philosophy.*" Darwin composed most of his works by writing his thoughts progressively wherever he happened to be. Harriet Beecher Stowe wrote her great masterpiece, "Uncle Tom's Cabin," while conducting other household activities. The worst thing about a lost hour is not so much the wasted time as the wasted power and knowledge.

> *"Let every man do that which is right, strive with all his might towards the goal which can never be obtained, develop to the last breath the gifts with which the gracious Creator has endowed him, and never cease to learn. For life is short, art eternal."* – LUDWIG VAN BEETHOVEN (1770-1827)

Start reflecting on how you spend your time after supper, on weekends, or on holidays and think about how you could use part of this time to expand your knowledge and pursue projects that would help you develop and learn from that experience. Try to learn something new each day, and make it a habit. Replace the time you normally spend on useless diversions with a constructive and developmental activity. Every hour counts. Waste of time means waste of energy, waste of curiosity, and waste of vitality. Lost time is gone forever and could lead to lost opportunities to achieve greater success in your life.

One important self-improvement trait that is critical in any walk of life is oratory skills. It does not matter whether you want to be a public speaker or not, everybody should have complete control of himself or herself, should be poised enough that he or she can get up in any audience, no matter how large, and express his or her thoughts clearly and distinctly. Self-expression brings out your best, highlighting your resourcefulness and creativity. No other form of self-expression develops a person so thoroughly and so effectively, and so quickly unfolds all of your powers, as expression before an audience.

Communication is about creating connections with the people you are interacting with. Whether you are selling an idea, a product or a concept, you must annihilate your self-consciousness and forget about yourself in your speech. In other words, stop wondering what kind of impression you are making or what people think of you during your conversations and speeches. Focus on what you have to convey, and adapt your style (in terms of speed and tone) based on the connections you are creating with your audience. From my own personal experience, the best speeches I gave or heard were those in which a connection was made with the audience. You will know instinctively that you are on the right track when you have built a bond that arouses interest and captures the audience, whether you are talking to one person or hundreds.

Maya Angelou said *"If you learn, teach; if you get, give."* The beauty of life is to be able to share and to be generous with your heart. As you follow the path of self-improvement, and as you teach others, you will be amazed how you will also learn from your students. In various circumstances this has proven true on a personal level. Whether I am teaching my daughter something new every day, or coaching people in various corporations, I am also learning a lot in the process. When my daughter was three years old, she was at the "Why?" phase. Everything we did, everything she saw and every answer we gave her was followed by the question "Why?" As we answered her questions in detail, she continued drilling us with more questions, reminding me that as adults we forget to ask ourselves these essential questions. Why do we choose certain paths in life? Why do we make certain decisions? Why do we choose one route instead of another? We must never forget to interrogate ourselves in order to discover new meaning in everything we do.

Another example where I learned an important lesson was through a team-building workshop I organized and which consisted in building bikes that would be donated to underprivileged kids. As the teams were divided, they had to answer trivia questions in order to obtain a bicycle part to build one. Each team was advised that they needed to validate their answers with three judges. The team members were not aware that the questions were divided among the three judges (I being one of the judges). Each judge could only provide confirmation to his or her questions. If a judge was provided with an answer that did not correspond to his or her question, all he/she could say was: "Sorry I cannot help you." When a team leader came to me with their answer to one of the trivia questions, and I answered "Sorry I cannot help you," in almost all cases, the team leader assumed the answer was wrong and simply went back for further deliberation. No matter how convinced they were that they had the right answer, they did not try to give the answer to other judges. After several trials, they eventually caught on, especially as the teams began sharing information, and they started putting the pieces together. It was amazing to see how we create our own limitations in the face of adversity. Life can bring many challenges. You must not let these challenges cloud your mind and stop you from acting. The answer may be at your finger tip, if only you could open your eyes to see it.

> *"The important thing is not to stop questioning. Curiosity has its own reason for existing. One cannot help but be in awe when he contemplates the mysteries of eternity, of life, of the marvelous structure of reality. It is enough if one*

tries merely to comprehend a little of this mystery every day. Never lose a holy curiosity." - ALBERT EINSTEIN (1879-1955)

Your abilities are limitless and you can expand your skills to an unimaginable potential, irrespective of your current situation or IQ. Francis Crick, the Nobel Prize Winner who co-discovered the structure for DNA, only had an IQ of 115, which is average. There is probably a hidden scientist or leader within you who simply needs a little effort to rise to the surface. In order to ensure you pursue a life of continuous self-improvement, follow the guidelines below:

- **Identify:** Identify what areas you wish to focus on for self-improvement. Do you wish to expand your general cultural knowledge, learn a new language or a new skill or obtain a new diploma? If there are many things you would like to do, choose one that is achievable in the short term. Focus on skills that are important to you, that come naturally, and that will allow you to achieve your ultimate life goal. Also, ask people who know you well and who have been very successful, what skills they suggest you develop. Also remember that the areas that are of interest to you today may evolve with time. Once you have started the self-improvement habit, you must continuously prioritize how you will allocate your time. Focus on expanding your skills in areas that come naturally to you, and that you know deep down you can be good at. Put priority in building your strengths rather than improving your weaknesses, since this will allow you to reach new heights much faster, and with more enjoyment. Furthermore, as mentioned earlier, I highly recommend making public speaking or oratory skills courses part of your priority list. Join as many self-improvement courses as you can and force yourself to speak every time you get a chance. If a chance does not come to you, make one. Every time you rise to your feet will increase your confidence, and after a while you will form the habit of speaking so that it will be as easy as anything else you do. Expressing your opinions with force and independence is similar to vigorous exercise for the mind, and is a must, irrespective of the field you are in.

- **Manage:** Organize your life in such a way that self-development becomes a habit. Analyze how you spend your free time and manage it so that every single day you learn something new. If you can dedicate fifteen minutes, thirty minutes or one hour per day, use this time to enrich yourself and expand your knowledge in a multitude of areas. If you do not manage your time well now and take control of your life, you may find yourself living a life of regret. There should be no more complaints or excuses for not finding time for self-improvement. You must either make time, or let life pass you by. Manage your performance, as any manager would, by building a system of **reward and punishment**. In other words, if you have decided to dedicate thirty minutes a day to development and you accomplish this during a week, reward yourself by doing something that you enjoy. If you have not dedicated the allocated time as per the original plan, do not allow yourself to do the activity you had planned. The system of reward and punishment, or the carrot and the stick, is a technique that works well in the corporate world, and that you can apply to your own life if managing your time becomes difficult.

- **Experience:** Learning is not just about theory but also about practice. You must be resourceful in finding ways to test and enhance your skills since there is nothing that compares to hands-on experience. Join an oratory or theatre club if you would like to enhance your speaking skills, volunteer your time to an organization that will allow you expand your knowledge in a specific area, or request to participate in a special project in your community or corporation in order to get hands-on experience. Do not be afraid of making mistakes, since the wealth of knowledge and experience you will achieve will make you stronger in the end.

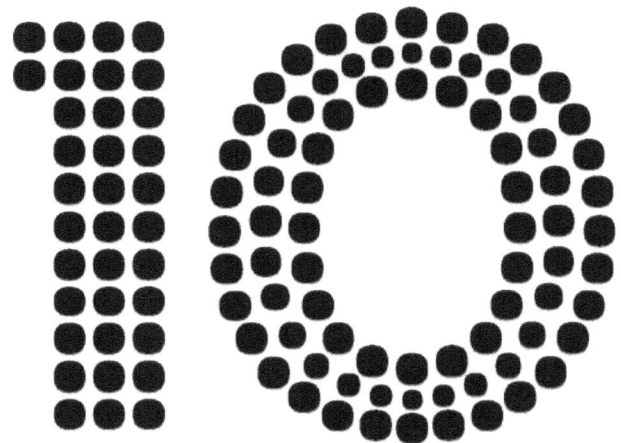

POSITIVE ATTITUDE

Positive thinking will lead to a bright future.

"Happiness is when what you think, what you say, and what you do are in harmony" – MAHATMA GANDHI (1869-1948)

"It is not in the stars to hold our destiny, but in ourselves" – WILLIAM SHAKESPEARE (1564-1616)

"He who is not contented with what he has, would not be contented with what he would like to have" – SOCRATES (469 BC-399 BC)

Is positive thinking reserved for the born optimists of this world? Can a person evolve into having a more positive perspective on life, or change from being a pessimist to being an optimist? According to Dr. Martin Seligman, in his book *"Learned Optimism – How to change your mind and your life,"* (Vintage Publishing, 2006) such changes are certainly possible. As he states, "One of the most significant findings in psychology in the last twenty years is that individuals can choose the way they think." Dr. Seligman believes that changing from a pessimistic outlook to an optimistic one is as easy as ABCDE. In his book he teaches how anyone can move from "**A**dversity" (seeing an event as negative), to "**B**elief" (understanding that you have control over how you interpret the adversity), to "**C**onsequence" (becoming aware of how your feel), to "**D**isputation" (asking yourself about the evidence, alternatives, implications, and usefulness of holding on to your old beliefs) and finally, once you have gone through these stages and have changed your negative thoughts, the stage called "Energization", wherein you actively turn negative and pessimistic thoughts into positive and optimistic ones.

Having a positive outlook on adverse events and having an overall positive attitude towards life and your ability to succeed will lead to a brighter future than maintaining thoughts that are clouded with pessimism. Not only will you be more energized, but you are likely to be healthier as well. Dr. Seligman references many studies in his book that have demonstrated, through research conducted around the world, that optimism can lead to a stronger immune system. Some of these studies span periods of thirty-five to sixty years, during which individuals were consistently evaluated in terms of health and success. Throughout the lifetime of these individuals, the research proved that a positive attitude led to more effective approaches to dealing with bad events in people's lives, and to healthier lives overall. And if you are healthier, you will have more strength and power to pursue the grand projects that will improve your life.

Life is short and I cannot imagine why you would not spend every moment smiling at how lucky you are to be alive, and being grateful that you have the power to create the world that you dream of. Albert Einstein used to say that *"there are only two ways to live your life. One is as though nothing is a miracle. The other is as though everything is a miracle."* The very fact that you are on this earth is a miracle, when you look at all the prerequisites for human creation. And the power you hold in your heart and soul to create anything you wish for is miraculous and almost magical. The secret is in finding control over your thoughts and ultimately your actions. Without positive thinking and a positive attitude towards life, your power as the creator of your success destiny evaporates. If you take every day for granted, and act as if you have plenty of time to start pursuing your dreams, think twice. Time flies, and before you know it, you will not have as much time as you thought in front of you. Build your life vision; be persistent in pursuing your goals; savor each day, joy and pleasure; and be generous with your heart towards those around you, since the highest happiness will always come from the exercise of the best things in you.

Generosity, charity and kindness are absolutely essential to real happiness. Those who are always covering up something, misleading, deceiving cannot get away from self-reproach, and hence cannot be really happy. Dishonesty in all its forms is fatal to happiness, for no dishonest person can attain self-approval. Before you can be really happy, you must be able to look back upon a life well-spent and a conscientious, unselfish past. In other words, **happiness is merely a result of your life work.** It is the harvest of your life effort, your habitual thought-processes and good deed-doing.

We all wear different-colored glasses and no two people see life with the same tint. Some find temporary happiness in various activities or sports, while others by simply reading a book. Some find their greatest happiness in friends, in financial success, in social networking, while others seek happiness in traveling around the world, always thinking that the greatest enjoyment is in another place. To many people, happiness is never where they are, but almost anywhere else. Most people lose sight of the simplicity of happiness and look for it in big, complicated things. Real happiness is perfectly simple, and simplicity is its very essence. Simple joys and the treasures of the heart and mind make true happiness. Happiness is a state of mind. The earliest you develop the happy habit, the habit of enjoying every day, no matter what comes your way, the more fulfilling and meaningful your life will be. Focus always on solutions rather than problems and on the positive in each situation, no matter how challenging it may be.

Real happiness cannot be obtained from things that pass away; it dwells only in principles, and in permanency. It is only in giving, in helping, that we attain our quest. The essence of happiness is honesty, sincerity, truthfulness. To be happy, we must be in tune with the infinite within us, in harmony with our better selves, like an orchestra whose instruments all work together to one tune. There is no happiness like that which comes from doing our best every day, and no satisfaction like that which comes from putting the stamp of superiority on everything which goes through our hands. The highest happiness is the feeling of wellbeing which comes to you when you are actively doing what you were made to do, carrying out your role of Chief Life Officer with a clear purpose, and having a sense of usefulness. We were all made to grow and to evolve. Nothing else can take the place of achievement in life. **Real happiness without achievement of some worthy aim is unthinkable**. One of the greatest satisfactions in this world is the feeling of growth, of stretching upward and onward that comes from accomplishment. Happiness is incompatible with stagnation. With growth there can be progress, and with progress success becomes achievable.

On the road to success, however, you may encounter challenges. If you ever experienced a bad period in your life, if you felt that your life was a failure, or if you made imprudent investments, wasted your time and money, do not let your past destroy your happiness. Stop wasting energy today over what cannot be changed. Don't let these old memories take any more of your vitality, waste any more of your time, or destroy any more of your happiness. There is only one thing to do with bitter experiences, blunders and unfortunate mistakes, or with memories that haunt you, and that is to forget them. Leave the past behind, and forget bitter memories. Close the door on everything in the past that causes pain and cannot help you. Free yourself from everything that keeps you from moving towards your dreams and makes you unhappy. Begin your days with a clean slate and a free mind. Don't be mortgaged to the past, since it will stop you from moving forward. Forget everything that has kept you back or has made you suffer, and never allow distressing memories to enter your mind again. Implement the ABCDE model mentioned earlier, and open the window to more happiness into your life. There is no doubt that your life was intended to be one grand, sweet symphony filled with sunshine and sublime melodies.

Do not be your own worst enemy. Everything depends upon your courage, your faith in yourself, in your holding a hopeful, optimistic outlook. If things go wrong or you have a discouraging day or an unfortunate experience, do not start tearing down your beliefs and destroying the life work that took you years to build up. Believe you are lucky and fortunate, and that all forces will turn in your favor. **You control your own destiny. Dream it and it will become real.** Live joyfully, celebrate and be thankful for what you have, and your fortune will continue growing. As the Swedish proverb goes, *"Fear less, hope more; Whine less, breathe more; Talk less, say more; Hate less, love more; and all good things are yours."*

You will find that as you increase confidence in yourself by the affirmation of what you wish to be and do, your ability will increase. No matter what other people may think about your ability, never allow yourself to doubt that you can do or become what you long for. Increase your self-confidence in every possible way, and you can do this to a remarkable degree by the power of self-suggestion. Affirm to yourself that you are an optimist—do not just think it; there is a force in words spoken aloud. Speaking your affirmation aloud will have a more lasting impression upon your mind, just as words which pass through the eye from the printed page make a greater impression on the brain than those same words if we only think them.

There are thousands of people who have lost everything they valued in the world, all the material results of their lives' endeavor, and yet, because they possess unconquerable spirits, a determination to push ahead which knows no retreat, they are as far from real failure as they were before their loss; and with such wealth they can never be poor. My parents lost all their belongings when we left Eastern Europe under the communist regime. In spite of all this, they kept saying: "No one can take away our pride, our knowledge, our joy for life and our belief that we will rebuild even a better future." They realized this dream, along with many others in similar circumstances.

Below are a few suggestions for continued positive thinking throughout your life:
- **Positive affirmations**: Force yourself to a higher standard every morning as you start your day, in the shower or as you are having breakfast. Have hard talks with yourself, and with stern discipline of this kind, you will be amazed by the results. Start out today with a firm resolution to make the returns from your work greater tonight than ever before. Do not say, "I shall be a success someday." Say, "I am a success. Success is my birthright." Do not say that you are going to be happy in the future. Say to yourself, "I was intended for happiness, made for it, and I am happy now." If, however, you affirm something but do not believe what you say, you will

not be helped by affirmation. You must believe what you affirm and realize it. Assert that you already possess the things you need, the qualities you long to have. Force your mind toward your goal, hold it there steadily, persistently, for this is the mental state that leads to creating your future. Say to yourself "I can create my future" and you will be amazed by the power these words will bring into your life. When negative thoughts emerge, force yourself to have two positive thoughts for each negative one, and you will develop a happier outlook on life.

- **Ignorance is bliss**: Look at information coming your way in terms of value. If it is negative, irrelevant to your goals, and outside of your control – ignore it. Sweep away all depressing thoughts, suggestions, all the rubbish that is troubling you. Start believing that no matter what happens, you are going to be happy. Form the habit of erasing from your mind all disagreeable and unhealthy thoughts. Start out every morning with a clean slate. Erase from your mental gallery all discordant and unpleasant pictures and replace them with harmonious, uplifting, life-giving ones.
- **Take care of your body:** By ensuring you get enough sleep, eat well, and exercise, you will naturally feel better and be more positive. In fact, when you exercise regularly, your body's metabolism regulates stress hormones like cortisol, and promotes the release of endorphins, which will naturally make you happier, and will give you a sense of accomplishment. By keeping a healthy body, you will naturally have more energy and vigor to pursue your goals.
- **Gratitude journal**: What is your "Theory of Enough?" In other words, what do you really need

to make yourself happy in terms of key basic and pleasurable necessities? We all need shelter, food, along with little pleasures. These may be music for some, dancing or wine or chocolate for others. Everything else is icing on the cake and a blessing. Count your blessings every day and record them in a journal. Psychologists have proven that gratitude journals can be effective happiness boosters. Since achieving success will mean different things for different people, your gratitude journal will reflect the essence of what makes you most happy. On the path to success, do not forget to celebrate the accomplishments made each day, no matter how small the achievement. Every step taken today will bring you closer to your goal tomorrow, so use your gratitude journal to elevate your spirits and to maintain a positive attitude as you move towards your goals.

FINAL REFLECTIONS

The ten secrets described in the previous chapters are all interdependent. Together they are your formula for success. If you truly want to achieve greatness personally and professionally, you will need to apply all the ten secrets consistently. You must first be clear about your vision and commit to becoming a great Chief Life Officer. If you then open your eyes to opportunities and ensure that every action you take is driven by excellence, your actions will quickly lead to success. Since every journey has its challenges, self-confidence and a positive attitude will be necessary to maintain your persistence.

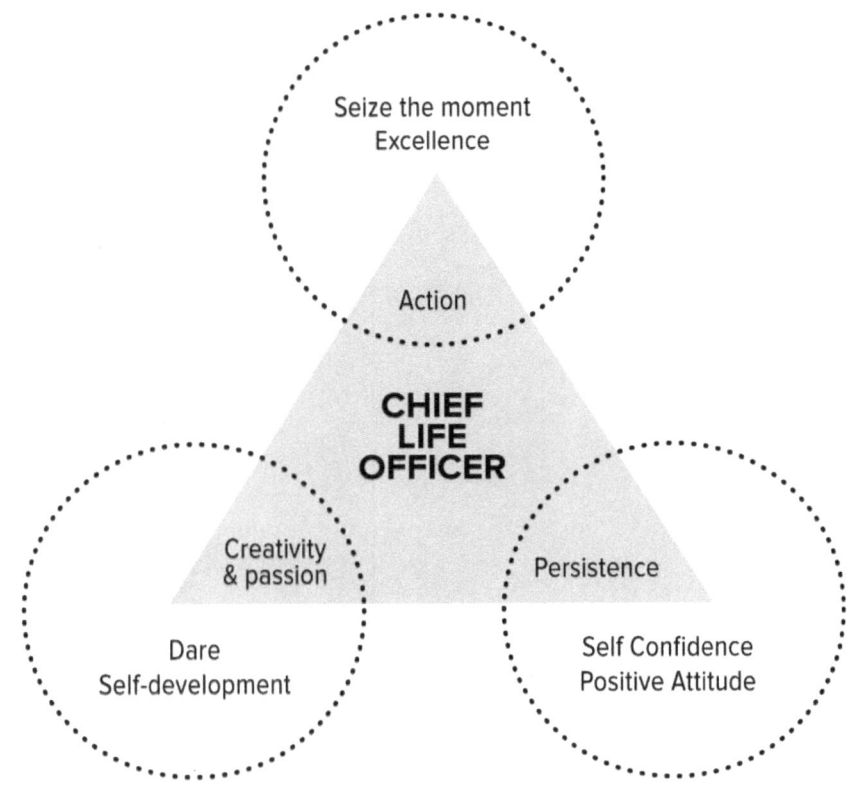

Finally, by leveraging your creativity and passion, your appetite for taking smart risks will widen, and your continuous self-development will lead you to expand your knowledge to new heights.

These ten secrets, exercised together, will lead you to a more enriching and successful life, irrespective of the path you choose to pursue. Only you can make the right choices for you on a personal and professional level. As your life evolves and you follow the ten secrets, you will achieve a strong Successonality, and, a fulfilling life without regrets.

From this day forward, you must always remember that:
> Your thoughts become words;
>
> Your words become your actions;
>
> Your actions become your habits;
>
> Your habits form your personality;
>
> Your personality will influence your destiny;
>
> And your destiny will be filled with success if you build your Successonality.

Be proud of what you have accomplished to date, and be daring in what you wish to accomplish tomorrow. Your Successonality is the key to your future success.

Do not waste valuable time. Begin right away and take your life to new heights!

BEGIN YOUR JOURNEY & SHARE YOUR STORY

Begin your Successonality journey today by visiting our website (**www.successonality.com**) to take the free **Successonality Assessment**. Your personalized Assessment will help you understand what has stopped you from realizing all your dreams in the past, and what you need to do to achieve your personal and professional goals in the future. The path to build your Successonality starts with this Assessment.

Share your story with us on how you have applied the ten secrets of Successonality to achieve your dreams. We would love to hear from you. Your story may be included on our website and other Successonality resources. Please send your email to **info@successonality.com**.

RESOURCES FOR PERSONAL GROWTH

Begin putting into action the Successonality principles by attending upcoming events in various cities around the world. Open your eyes to your hidden powers, and unleash the strength that you need to begin moving towards your dreams.

The Successonality personal growth events will provide you with the skills necessary to reach your highest potential and inspire you to pursue your dreams.

- Learn how to apply the ten secrets of Successonality to achieve any goal

- Discover how to build your strategies and action plan to succeed personally and professionally

- Find out how to turn challenges into opportunities

- Overcome barriers and limitations to reach phenomenal results

- Discover your hidden powers and learn how to embrace your role as Chief Life Officer

- Have fun and build lasting relationships with other attendees

Please consult **www.successonality.com** for details on event locations and dates.

For personal coaching services, please contact us at **info@successonality.com**.

RESOURCES FOR CORPORATIONS

Build a Successonality focused corporation with a tailored event that is focused on the key strategic areas most important to you. For executives and teams, our events will provide you with the foundations to build a more profitable and effective corporation. Empower your team to exceed targets, and build a company that stands out from its competitors.

For more information, or to book a Successonality event for your company, please visit **www.successonality.com** or contact us at **info@successonality.com.**

SPREAD THE WORD

Help us enrich the lives of others by sharing the Successonality secrets with friends and colleagues. Encourage them to visit the website (**www.successonality.com**), and suggest that they take the Assessment in order to obtain their current success blueprint based on the ten secrets of Successonality.

Write a book review on sites such as Amazon.com, and share your thoughts with others on Facebook, Twitter, or your blog, if you have one.

Ask your local TV station, radio or online media to have the author interviewed to share the principles of Successonality, in order to help everyone build a life filled with personal and professional successes.

ABOUT THE AUTHOR

Andreea Vanacker, is the founder and CEO of Successonality Inc., and a leading expert in empowering individuals to achieve extraordinary success personally and professionally. She has inspired people worldwide to achieve their dreams by embracing the ten secrets of Successonality, and has helped corporations build motivated teams that excel in terms of results. Prior to becoming an author and a speaker, she managed multi-million dollar businesses in the technology, aviation and consumer goods industries, and worked extensively internationally. Andreea holds a Doctorate degree in Economics.

For more information visit:

www.successonality.com

www.ingramcontent.com/pod-product-compliance
Lightning Source LLC
Chambersburg PA
CBHW022107160426
43198CB00008B/379